TELEPEN
D0411079
35293
62386

Published by
The Talbot Adair Press
Newlands, Pewley Hill
Guildford, Surrey GU1 3SN, England

ISBN 0 9511835 8 3

Phototypeset by Primagraphics, Camberley.
Printed and bound in Great Britain by
Biddles Ltd, Guildford and King's Lynn

UNDERSTANDING MOTIVATION

John Adair

TALBOT
ADAIR
PRESS

UNDERSTANDING MOTIVATION

Books by John Adair

LEADERSHIP AND MANAGEMENT

Training for Leadership
Training for Decisions
Training for Communication
Action-Centred Leadership
Management and Morality
The Becoming Church
Effective Leadership
Management Decision-Making
Effective Teambuilding
How to Manage Your Time
Not Bosses But Leaders
Developing Leaders
Great Leaders
The Art of Creative Thinking
The Challenge of Innovation

HISTORY

Hastings to Culloden (with Peter Young)
Roundhead General
Cheriton, 1644
John Hampden
The Pilgrims' Way
Royal Palaces of Britain
Founding Fathers
By the Sword Divided

Contents

The two great movers of the human mind are the desire of good, and the fear of evil.

Samuel Johnson

Introduction

What motivates people — what makes them tick — is a subject of perennial fascination. It is especially important for practical leaders in industry, commerce and the public services — and indeed to anyone who works with other people — to think about this question in some depth.

What is motivation? A man or woman is motivated when he or she WANTS to do something. A motive is not quite the same as an incentive. Whereas a person may be inspired or made enthusiastic by an incentive, his or her main motive for wanting to do something may be fear of punishment. Motivation covers ALL the reasons which underlie the way in which a person acts.

Two American professors of psychology — Abraham Maslow and Frederick Herzberg — have made major contributions to our understanding of motivation. Our common phrase 'job satisfaction' arose largely from the work of the latter. Maslow is now the world's most influential psychologist after Freud and Jung. The time is ripe for a review of their contributions to motivational theory in the light of the needs of the 1990s.

In my judgement no other comparable studies of motivation to those of Maslow and Herzberg have emerged from other authors. Or, rather, they have emerged but not stayed the course. Maslow and Herzberg have stood the test of time. This fact does not, of course, guarantee them, but it does at least suggest that there is a large element of truth in them. For, as Albert Einstein once said, 'Truth is that which stands the test of experience.'

This book goes beyond Maslow and Herzberg, however, and it offers a new general theory of motivation. My reflections on Maslow and Herzberg over the years, in the context of developing the Action-Centred Leadership (ACL) model, have led me to formulate the Fifty-Fifty Rule. Put simply, it proposes that fifty per cent of our motivation is inner-generated, while fifty per cent comes from outside of us.

The real point of the book, of course, is to stimulate your own thought and ideas on this most interesting of all subjects. It should lead you to see some practical ways in which you can better motivate yourself and others.

PART ONE

Leadership and Motivation

1 Action-Centred Leadership

Leadership is action, not position.
Donald H. McGannon

Leadership and motivation are like brother and sister. It is difficult to think of a leader who does not motivate others. But leadership embraces more than motivation.

What is leadership? The Action-Centred Leadership (ACL) approach offers a comprehensive answer to that question. The model encompasses the concept of Individual Needs, which is the area charted by Maslow and Herzberg. Therefore it provides a natural context for an exploration of their theories in Part Two. In this chapter I shall outline the original content of ACL.

THE BACKGROUND

Functional Leadership training was first developed in the early 1960s at the Royal Military Academy, Sandhurst as part of a programme introducing young officer cadets to the responsibilities of leadership. When transposed by The Industrial Society into industry and commerce in the early 1970s it was renamed Action-Centred Leadership (ACL).

Initially, while I was directly involved myself with The Industrial Society — first as Assistant Director and Head of the Leadership Department in 1969 and later as Associate Director for three years — the core content of ACL remained much the same as the original Sandhurst version, though the practical exercises and case studies were changed. After 1973, however, that content was gradually altered and attenuated, until today The Industrial Society's ACL courses now bear little resemblance to my original concept.

In this introductory chapter I shall present the framework of that original concept of ACL, and then comment upon its constituent elements in the following chapter. In order to do so I have drawn upon the relevant chapters in *Training for Leadership* (1968) and *Action-Centred Leadership* (1973), my first and second books on the subject.

My standard introduction to the ACL model has been to look first at the Qualities Approach and then at the Situational Approach to leadership. Having outlined these approaches or theories, identifying both their drawbacks and their positive contributions to our understanding of leadership, I moved on to the third ingredient in any story (apart from the personality and character of the *leader* and the *situation* in which it was all happening), namely the *people* concerned. Having mentioned the amount of research done on groups as wholes that are more than the sum of their parts (which led to the establishment of the new sub-discipline of Social Psychology) I explain that I have selected one theory from the mass of research material which I consider to be of most relevance to the practical manager intent upon understanding leadership and motivation — the theory of *group needs*. To this I add the concept of *group personality*. This is how I actually explain it.

THE THEORY OF GROUP PERSONALITY AND GROUP NEEDS

As a starting point I have developed the idea that working groups resemble individuals in that although they are always unique (each develops its own 'group personality') yet they share, as do individuals, certain common 'needs'. There are three areas of need present in such groups. Two of these are the properties of the group as a whole, namely *the need to accomplish the common task* and *the need to be maintained as a cohesive social unity* (which I have called the 'team maintenance need'). The third area is constituted by the sum of the *individual needs* of group members.

INDIVIDUAL NEEDS AND MOTIVATION

This third area of need present in the corporate life inheres in the individual members rather than in the group itself. To the latter they bring a variety of needs — physical, social, intellectual and spiritual — which may or may not be met by participating in the activity of the group. Probably physical needs first drew men together in working groups: the primitive hunter could take away from the slain elephant a hunk of meat and a piece of hide for his own family. Nowadays the means for satisfying these basic needs of food, shelter and protection are received in money rather than in kind, but the principle remains the same.

There are, however, other needs less tangible or conscious even to their possessors which the social interaction of working together in groups may or may not fulfil. These tend to merge into one another, and they cannot be isolated with any precision, but Figure 1.1 will indicate their character. Drawn from the work of A. H. Maslow[1] it also makes the point that needs are organized on a priority basis. As basic needs become relatively satisfied the higher needs come to the fore and become motivating influences.

Physiological	Safety	Social	Esteem	Self actualization
Hunger	Security	Belonging	Self respect	Growth
Thirst	Protection from danger	Social activities	Status	Personal development
Sleep		Love	Recognition	Accomplishment

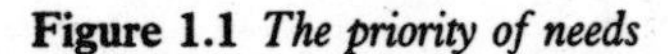

Figure 1.1 *The priority of needs*

These needs spring from the depths of our common life as human beings. They may attract us to, or repel us from, any given group. Underlying them all is the fact that people need one another, not just to survive but to achieve and develop personality. This growth occurs in a whole range of social activity – friendship, marriage, neighbourhood – but inevitably work groups are extremely important because so many people spend so much of their waking time in them.

Professor Frederick Herzberg has dichotomized the list by suggesting that the factors which make people experience satisfaction in their work situation are not the reverse of those which make them dissatisfied. The latter is caused by deficiencies in the environment or context of the job; in contrast, job satisfaction rests upon the content of the work and the opportunities it presents for achievement, recognition, professional development, and personal growth.[2]

THE NEEDS INTERACT

The first major point is that these three areas of need influence one another for better or worse. For example, if a group fails in its task this will intensify the disintegrative tendencies present in the group and produce a diminished satisfaction for its individual members. If there is a lack of unity or harmonious relationships in the group this will affect performance on the job and also individual needs (cf. A. H. Maslow's Social Needs). And obviously an individual who feels frustrated and unhappy in a particular work environment will not make his maximum contribution to either the common task or to the life of the group.

Conversely, achievement in terms of a common aim tends to build a sense of group identity — the 'we-feeling', as some have called it. The moment of victory closes the psychological gaps between people: morale rises naturally. Good internal communications and a developed team spirit based upon past successes make a group much more likely to do well in its task area, and incidentally provide a more satisfactory climate for the individual. Lastly, an individual whose needs are recognized and who feels that he or she can make a characteristic and worthwhile contribution both to the task and the group will tend to produce good fruits in both these areas.

We can illustrate these interrelations with a simple model:

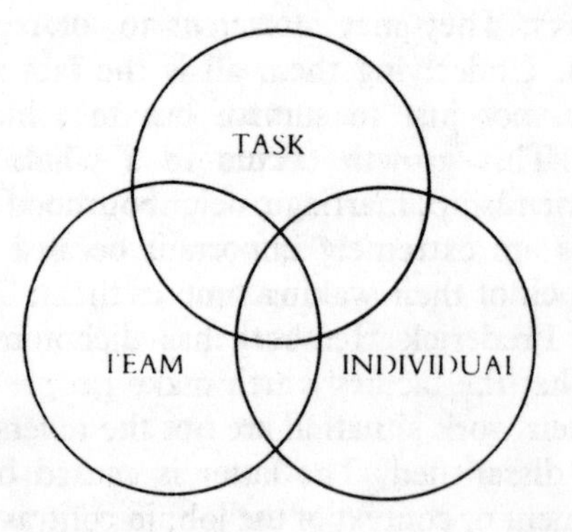

Figure 1.2 *Interaction of Needs*

If you place a coin over the 'Task' circle it will immediately cover segments of the other two circles as well. In other words, lack of task or failure to achieve it will affect both team maintenance, e.g. increasing disruptive tendencies, and also the area of individual needs, lowering member satisfaction within the group. Move the coin on to the 'Team' circle, and again the impact of a near-complete lack of relationships in the group on both task and individual needs may be seen at a glance.

Conversely, when a group achieves its task the degree of group cohesiveness and enjoyment of membership should go up. Morale, both corporate and individual, will be higher. And if the members of a group happen to get on extremely well together and find that they can work closely as a team, this will increase their work performance and also meet some important needs which individuals bring with them into the common life.

These three interlocking circles therefore illustrate the general point that each area of need exerts an influence upon the other two: they do not form watertight compartments.

LEADERSHIP FUNCTIONS

In order for the needs in these areas to be met in any group or organization certain *functions* have to be performed. According to this integrated theory the provision of these necessary functions is the responsibility of leadership, although that does not imply that the leader will perform all of them himself or herself. Indeed, in groups over the size of about five members there are too many functions required for any one person to supply them all himself.

Various attempts have been made to list the functions in recent years, but they suffer from several disadvantages. In the first place, some researchers have produced three separate lists, one for each area. The difference between 'Task' and 'Team Maintenance' is always in danger of yawning into a dichotomy. The value of the three *overlapping* circles is that they emphasize the essential unity of leadership: a single action can be multi-functional in that it touches all three areas. The distinction between the circles should not therefore be pressed too far, and separate lists favour that unfortunate tendency. Secondly, many of the lists reflect the 'group dynamics laboratory' situation too much. Thirdly, it is rather artificial to categorize the response of leaders to individual needs. It is sufficient to recognize that effective leaders are aware of this dimension, and respond in appropriate ways with understanding. Such action might range from changing the content of an individual's job or role, along the lines advocated by Professor Herzberg, to a promotion or a word of encouragement.

It is perhaps best to work out a single list of leadership functions within the context of a given working situation, so that the sub-headings can have the stamp of reality upon them. But there is general agreement upon the essentials, and to illustrate some of these major functions meeting the three interacting areas of need, I give here a list originally worked out at the Royal Military Academy, Sandhurst, which has been the basis for numerous adaptations in industry and other fields:

- *Planning*: e.g. Seeking all available information.
  Defining group task, purpose or goal.
  Making a workable plan (in right decision-making framework).
- *Initiating*: e.g. Briefing group on the aims and the plan.
  Explaining why aim or plan is necessary.
  Allocating tasks to group members.
  Setting group standards.
- *Controlling*: e.g. Maintaining group standards.
  Influencing tempo.
  Ensuring al' actions are taken towards objectives.
  Keeping discussion relevant.
  Prodding group to action/decision.
- *Supporting*: e.g. Expressing acceptance of persons and their contribution.
  Encouraging group/individuals.
  Disciplining group/individuals.
  Creating team spirit.
  Relieving tension with humour.
  Reconciling disagreements or getting others to explore them.
- *Informing*: e.g. Clarifying task and plan.
  Giving new information to the group, i.e. keeping them 'in the picture'.

Receiving information from group.
Summarizing suggestions and ideas coherently.
- *Evaluating*: e.g. Checking feasibility of an idea.
  Testing the consequences of a proposed solution.
  Evaluating group performance.
  Helping the group to evaluate its own performance against standards.

SHARING DECISIONS

Without forgetting the broader opportunities open to members for supplementing the work of leadership in all three areas described above it is especially useful to examine specifically the extent to which the leader should share with others the general function of *decision-making*, the core of such more definite functions as setting objectives and planning.

In an invaluable diagram R. Tannenbaum and W. H. Schmidt[3] plotted the possibilities of participation. The diagram can be compared to a cake: at one end the leader has virtually all of it, and at the other the group has the lion's share. In terms of a transaction between a leader and an individual follower the continuum also illustrates the degrees of delegation that are possible in the context of a given decision.

There is much to be said for moving as far to the right of the continuum as possible, for the more that people share in decisions which directly affect them the more they are motivated to carry them out – providing they trust the integrity of the leader who is inviting them to participate in the decision. Yet factors in the *situation* (especially the nature of the task and the time available for the decision) and the *group* (especially the attitudes, knowledge, and experience of members) will naturally limit the extent to which the right-hand edge of the continuum can be approached. Other limiting factors may be present in the personality of the leader or the value system and philosophy of a particular organization, factors which cannot be described as natural or intrinsic in the same way as the situational or group constraints.

There are some groups and organizations whose *characteristic* working situations (as contrasted to the actual ones they may be in for ninety per cent of their time) are essentially crisis ones, where by definition time is short for decisions and the matter of life or death rests upon prompt decisions from one man e.g. operating theatre teams, fire brigades, police forces, airline crews, and military organizations. Yet such groups are not always in crisis situations, and for training purposes, if for no other reason, they need to explore the decision-making scale. Moreover, although it is not always possible to share decisions over *ends* (i.e. goals, objectives, aims or purpose) it is usually possible to involve others more or less fully in *means* (i.e. methods, techniques, conditions, and plans).

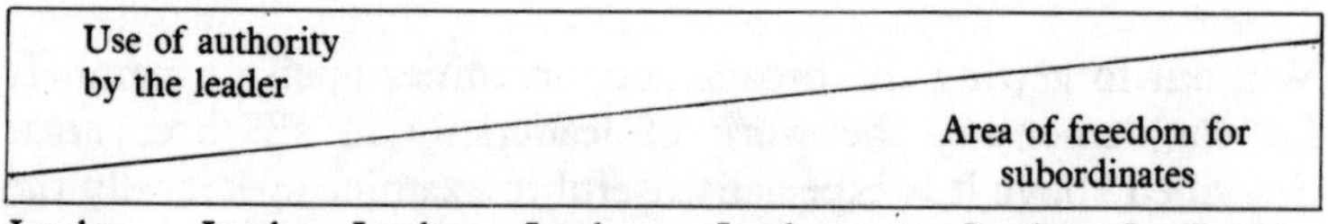

Use of authority by the leader

Area of freedom for subordinates

Leader makes decision and announces it	Leader 'sells' decision	Leader presents ideas & invites questions	Leader presents tentative decision subject to change	Leader presents problem, gets suggestions, makes decision	Leader defines limits; asks group to make decision	Leader permits subordinates to function within limits defined by superior

Figure 1.3 *A Continuum of Shared Decisions*

Rather than engaging in the fruitless attempt to establish a particular spot or 'style' on the scale which is 'best' we should see the continuum as a sliding scale, or as a thermometer marked with boiling and freezing points.[4] Where the latter points fall on the scale will depend upon the characteristic working situation of the group or organization. There will be a difference, for example, between an earth-shifting gang of labourers constructing a motorway and a research group in an electronics or chemical firm.

CONCLUSION

We can now construct a general idea or integrated concept of a leader as a person with certain *qualities* of personality and character, which are appropriate to the general *situation* and supported by a degree of relevant technical knowledge and experience, who is able to provide the necessary *functions* to guide a group towards the further realization of its purpose, while maintaining and building its unity as a team; doing all this in the right ratio or proportion with the contributions of other members of the team. The length of this last sentence clearly precludes it from ever becoming a neat definition, but it is a framework for drawing together the major strands of research into the nature of leadership without exhausting the inherent mystery present in it as in all human relations.

2 The ACL Model in Perspective

Most of the changes we think we see in life are merely truths going in or out of fashion.
Robert Frost

The model at the core of Action-Centred Leadership (ACL) – the three overlapping circles of Task, Team and Individual – is rapidly becoming one of the most widely taught management theories in the world. Its simplicity, coupled with its proven track record as a basis for leadership training courses, commends it to management developers. Some sophisticated trainers are using it to integrate a number of other concepts, ideas and practices which can be grouped under the heading of 'the human side of enterprise'. The ACL model is emerging in management studies, in effect, as something akin to Einstein's General Theory of Relativity. For it does identify the three main forces at work in working groups and organizations, and it charts (by way of a Venn diagram of the three circles) their main interrelationships with a degree of predictive accuracy.

THE WIDER ACL MODEL

This simplicity, however, is deceptive. True simplicity is different from the simplistic or superficial. Einstein's words warn us against such a reduction: 'Everything should be made as simple as possible, but not more simple.'

As this book reveals, the three-circle model contains surprising depths of meaning to those who are willing to think and reflect about it. But it is a great mistake to reduce my original concept of ACL down to just the three circles, however central and pivotal they may be to the whole. Many books which reproduce the three circles, and many organizations that purport to teach

ACL, do tend to pick out the three-circles diagram because it is so distinctive. But they then skate over, or leave out altogther, other ingredients in the original ACL complex of ideas which I regard as essential. This can lead to distortion.

Indeed the originality of ACL lay not in its parts — none of them were actually brought into their first existence by me — but in their integration into a whole which is more than their parts and in the application of them to training. By being brought into a new relation with one another those parts have undergone varying degrees of transformation, which is inevitable in any creative work.

But they have not lost their identity. And it has been my habit to name the parts and discuss them when talking to professional audiences.

THE ELEMENTS OF ACL

Let me now list for you the constituent parts of the wider ACL general theory, as a preface to commenting briefly upon some of them:

- Qualities Approach to Leadership.
- Situational Approach to Leadership.
- Group or Functional Approach to Leadership.
- Task, Group (or Team) and Individual Needs.
- The Theories of Maslow and Herzberg on motivation (in relation to the Individual Needs circle).
- The Three-Circles Model.
- How the circles — or areas of need — interact.
- Functions of Leadership.
- How far should leadership be shared? In the Task area, for example, how far should the leader share decisions? The Tannenbaum and Schmidt model.
- Drawing the threads together: the integrated functional (or ACL) concept of leadership.

Since the inception of ACL some thirty years ago that framework has been constant. That is what I have taught, in season and out of season. But in the outside world the parts themselves (which I may remind you were self-evidently not my own creations) have suffered varying changes. They have fallen from vogue or risen again as fashions change. Let us look at some of these changes as measured against the constant message of ACL.

THE QUALITIES APPROACH

The Qualities Approach, for example, was universally unpopular in the 1950s and 1960s among management theorists and social psychologists. The idea that leadership might characterize one person rather than another, not least because he or she possessed leadership qualities, was then deeply unfashionable in America among social scientists (as they liked to be called) for cultural reasons. The ACL general theory was virtually unique in those days in retaining it as a contributory source to our understanding of leadership.

The false assumptions latent in the American understanding of leadership were indeed challenged by a few individuals, notably William H. Whyte in *The Organizational Man* (1955). A decade later A. H. Maslow visited several organizations in California and commented:

> 'What I smell here is again some of the democratic dogma and piety in which all people are equal and in which the conception of a factually strong person or natural leader or dominant person or superior intellect or superior decisiveness or whatever is bypassed because it makes everybody uncomfortable and because it seems to contradict the democratic philosophy (of course, it does *not* really contradict it).'[1]

It took more than another decade before American behavioural scientists, such as Warren Bennis and Bernard Bass, backtracked to the Qualities Approach. From about 1975 onwards a spate of books on leadership has poured from the American presses discussing the qualities required in leaders. In a sense this change of heart was market-led. What happened? Organizations in the grips of change began to look for leadership from their chief executives. They needed someone with a sense of direction at the helm to guide them through the stormy waters of uncertainty. One or two American writers began to study the qualities of such leaders as Lee Iacocca at Chrysler or Jack Welch of General

Electric and suddenly the floodgates were opened and it was permissible once more in America to speak about leaders as unusual or gifted individuals.

In original ACL theory the first principle about the qualities of leaders suggests that they tend to possess (or should exemplify) the *qualities expected or admired in their work groups*. Physical courage, for example, does not make you into a military leader, but you cannot be one without it. A large part of the popularity of President Reagan, to give a second example, stemmed from the fact that many Americans saw him as personifying the core American characteristics and values. This point does suggest a powerful link between leadership and given work situations (such as engineering, nursing, or teaching), and may help to explain why the transfer of leadership from one field to another is often so difficult.

The British tradition on leadership has always emphasized the moral qualities of a good leader, such as moral courage and integrity. I cannot recollect ever talking about leadership without mentioning the importance of *integrity*. For, as Lord Slim said, integrity is the quality which makes people trust you. 'Trust being lost,' wrote the Roman historian Livy, 'all the social intercourse of men is brought to naught.'

From the beginning I also suggested that *enthusiasm* was a leadership quality, simply because I could not think of any leader I had met or read about who lacked it. Again, research over the last thirty years has amply confirmed that intuitive conclusion.

What I suggested at the end of the section on the Qualities Approach in my seminars was that you could – and should – go on thinking about the qualities of leadership for the rest of your life. There are always more facets of the diamond. Each leader you encounter may exhibit some particular quality or combination of qualities.

One particular methodological problem over qualities research has now been solved. The early American researchers compared some of the lists of qualities – such as initiative, perseverance, courage – which emerged from empirical research on leadership in order to see which words appeared on all or most lists. They found little or no agreement. For example, one classic survey of twenty experimental studies, made in 1940, revealed that only five per cent of the leadership qualities examined were common to four or more studies. High intelligence came top; it appeared in ten lists, followed by initiative which was mentioned in six of them. As there are some seventeen thousand words in the English language relating to personality and character there seemed to be plenty of choice and ample margin for error. These researchers were in fact victims of what philosophers have called the *word-concept fallacy*. Two words — such as *perseverance* and *persistence* — may be different, but they belong to the same family of meaning, the same concept. The researchers should have been fishing with wider meshed nets. For they should have been seeking clusters of meanings or concepts.

The mention of *integrity* on ACL courses has often provoked interesting discussions about the values of leadership. Was Hitler a good leader? How about Genghis Khan? What the research which went into my book *Great Leaders* (1989) has shown is that the English tradition concerning leadership (from whence sprang the American tradition) was fundamentally moral in complexion. Both the Graeco-Roman leadership tradition and the Biblical-Christian leadership tradition carried moral genes with them when grafted onto the existing tribal tradition of the nascent European nations. They held up the ideal of being a good leader and a leader for good.

It is true that a different message emanated from Machiavelli in the sixteenth century, but this godless Italian doctrine was never accepted into the mainstream of the Western tradition concerning leadership. The moral qualities approach-based upon Aristotle's four virtues: justice, prudence, fortitude and temperance — was far too deep-seated. Even in *The Path to Leadership* (1961) Field-Marshal Lord Montgomery could refer with approval to them. For this reason leaders in the Western culture who pursue immoral ends, or employ cynical, Machiavellian manipulation to achieve their ends, are unlikely to enjoy more than a brief success. Hitler did not last.

THE SITUATIONAL APPROACH

The situational approach, or contingency theory as it is now called, enjoyed a vogue in the 1960s mainly as a result of the work of Professor F. E. Fiedler of the University of Illinois and his associates. They studied the extent to which leadership veered towards the two poles of 'task oriented' and 'considerate' (or 'human relations') and tried to predict the circumstances in which one of these leadership 'styles' would be more effective than the other. Factors such as group composition, the degree of structuring in the task, and the 'position power' of the leader came into play. Fiedler believed that: 'We can improve the effectiveness of leadership by accurate diagnosis of the group-task situation and by altering the leader's work environment.'[2]

Like so many ideas and models, despite much revised work on the variables in the situation, Fiedler's work does not seem to have stood the test of time. It is now of little interest, except to specialists in psychological research. But of course the idea that the influence of the situation pervades leadership is by no means out-of-date. ACL theory has always made four points under the heading of the Situational Approach:

- Situations are partly constant and partly variable. For example, working in a bank has a continuity and a uniqueness compared with, say, working in a hospital. This is true of all fields, for they are all *unique*. But there has been much change in banking (as in all other fields). So it's a partly constant, partly changing situation.
- Leaders personify or exemplify (or should do so) the qualities expected or required in their working groups. This principle clearly links leadership to particular working situations.
- The Situational Approach highlights the importance of *knowledge* in leadership. There are three forms of authority in human affairs: the authorities of position, knowledge and personality. The latter in its extreme form is what is correctly called charisma. Knowledge is especially important. As the proverb says, 'Authority flows to him who knows.' As I discovered in writing *Great Leaders* (1989), it was Socrates who advanced for the first time the theory that knowledge was the key to the door of leadership.
- Some people, however, who acquire considerable technical or professional knowledge, and are specialists in a particular kind of work, are not perceived

> by their colleagues or subordinates as leaders. In other words, there is more to leadership than technical knowledge. It is this more general or transferable aspect that the Qualities Approach attempted — with only partial success — to analyze and define.

In summarizing at the end of a talk on leadership I have usually made the point that a leader should possess knowledge, which will be partly technical or specialist and partly general. The more general leadership or management knowledge will include: an understanding of people and what motivates them; some knowledge of the Qualities, Situational and Functional Approaches to leadership; some knowledge of the processes of effective thinking in its three applied forms — decision-making, problem-solving and creative thinking — so that one can guide a group in the process of making a decision, solving a problem or having new ideas; and, lastly, some knowledge about the principles and practice of good communication at inter-personal, group and organizational levels. Of course I am using 'knowledge' here to mean not only 'knowing about' in an academic sense of knowing facts, but the knowledge that can only be expressed in what you do and what you are.

Where does that leave us over the key issue of transfer? ACL theory suggests that a leader should have some degree of technical or professional knowledge. (That, incidentally, sets it apart from one popular version of the concept of management, which assumes that a manager once trained is equipped to manage in any kind of organization.)

It's a question of level really. At the lower level of leadership (to use a hierarchical analogy), technical or professional knowledge is clearly very important. Nobody is going to respect a leader who manifestly does not know what he or she is talking about. The leader of an orchestra, for example, must be able to play the violin and lead the strings. Higher up, where the more general kinds of leadership knowledge become more important, the degree of technical or specialist knowledge required is smaller although none-the-less important. The conductor of an orchestra, to continue that example, does not have to be a good instrumentalist.

Transfer *within* a general field, such as industry or commerce, must be contrasted to transfer *between* general fields, such as military to politics, or industry to hospitals. Obviously the former is relatively more easy. A chief executive moving from company to company takes with him or her (or should do so) a transferable cluster of leadership skills – including decision-making and communication know-how – and also a transferable cluster of business abilities, notably in finance and marketing. All that remains to be learnt is the particular technology involved in the product or service. What matters now is speed of learning. A good strategic leader will soon acquire all that he or she needs to know. Lack of background knowledge can be turned into an advantage in so far as it keeps you out of the engine room when you should be on the bridge. Getting involved unnecessarily in detail is one of the failings of those who rise to the top in their own fields.

INDIVIDUAL NEEDS

As far as I know, Maslow did not himself actually use a diagram to illustrate his hierarchy of needs. The familiar model in the shape of a pyramid must therefore have been a later addition, but it is now commonplace in text books on management.

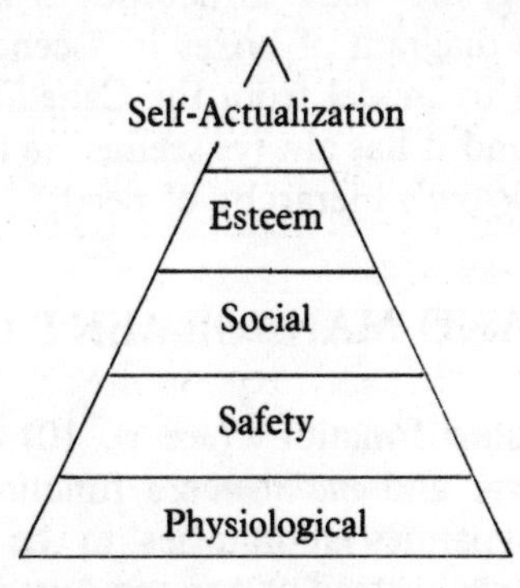

Figure 2.1 *The Pyramid Model of Human Needs*

Unfortunately this way of presenting Maslow's hierarchy makes it look as if our greatest needs are in the lower ranges, and that they narrow in size as you progress up the pyramid. But physiological needs, for example, are limited: you can only eat so many meals a day. In fact there are less limitations the further up you go. Therefore, if you persist with the pyramid model, it makes more sense to invert it thus:

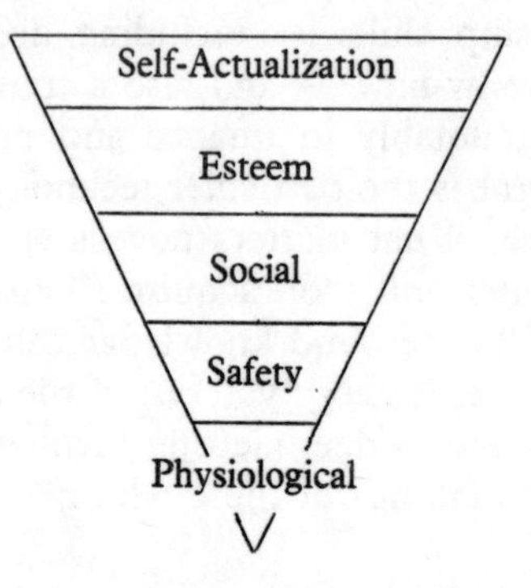

Figure 2.2 *The Inverted Pyramid of Human Needs*

I have left the diagram open-ended at the top in order to suggest that there may be another level of need beyond self-actualization, namely the need to transcend oneself. As we shall see later, Maslow virtually reached that important conclusion himself towards the end of his life.

Be that as it may, the visual difficulties of the pyramid in its are obviated if the diagram of boxes in ascending size (p. 7) is used. I borrowed this model from the Canadian Armed Forces in the mid-1960s, and it has always seemed to me the better way of representing Maslow's hierarchy of needs.

LEADERSHIP AND MANAGEMENT FUNCTIONS

The list of leadership functions (see p. 10) originated as my synthesis of the *task* and *maintenance* functions taught in the American 'group dynamics laboratories' in the late 1950s. Apart from being in two lists instead of one the American compilations had the added disadvantage I have mentioned already, namely that they were redolent of the 'group laboratory' situation: leaderless groups with no other goal but 'to become a group' over a two-week period. As I was using the functional list as a basis for training real leaders in real situations the list had to be made generally applicable. For example, a function such as *summarizing* assumes importance in leading a discussion-group, but it is a relatively minor skill if one is looking at the leadership functions required in a strategic leader.

The connection between the list that I produced from these sources and Henri Fayol's classic list of functions was soon noted.

Fayol, who was born in 1841, was a French mining engineer and became the director of a large group of coal pits before retiring in 1918. He published *General and Industrial Administration* two years earlier, but the first English translation of it did not appear until 1949. In it Fayol divided the activities of an industrial company into six main groups:

Technical	—production, manufacture, adaptation.
Commercial	—buying, selling, exchange.
Financial	—search for an optimum use of capital.
Security	—protection of property and people.
Accounting	—stocktaking, balance sheet, costs, statistics.
Administration	—forecasting and planning, organizing, commanding, co-ordinating and controlling.

Fayol defined command as 'getting the organization going' and he gives some examples of what it means in practice. A person in command should:

- Have a thorough knowledge of employees.
- Eliminate the incompetent.
- Be well versed in the agreements binding the business and its employees.
- Set a good example.
- Conduct periodic audits of the organization and use summarized charts to further this review.
- Bring together his chief assistants by means of conferences at which unity of direction and focusing of effort are provided for.
- Not become engrossed in detail.
- Aim at making unity, energy, initiative and loyalty prevail among all employees.

Fayol's analysis of managing in terms of functions has withstood more than a half century of critical discussion. L. F. Urwick, an early British exponent of Fayol's theory, in his *The Elements of Administration* (1947), made use of the more appropriate English word leadership for this aspect of management.

The ACL general theory provides a natural framework for Fayol's pioneering work. In it Fayol's list of functions could be developed in such a way as to ensure that all three areas of need — task, team or group, and individual — are met. It points out that a classic function such as *planning*, which may seem to be merely a task function, in fact influences both the other areas of need for good or ill. Moreover, Fayol is brought up-to-date by the addition of some more general functions in the team-building and team maintenance area, as well as functional responses to the individual needs circle.

THE DECISION-MAKING CONTINUUM

The Tannenbaum and Schmidt continuum, which first appeared in the *Harvard Business Review*, was always integral to the ACL general theory. It has a direct link with motivation for the reason given, namely that *the more that people share in a decision which affects their working life the more they tend to be motivated to carry it out*. This is a fundamental principle in motivation.

In America after 1960 (the date when I first encountered it there) the Tannenbaum and Schmidt chart slipped gradually into relative obscurity. The authors did produce a revised version of it in the *Harvard Business Review*, but their second thoughts obscured rather than enhanced the value of the original model.

Tannenbaum and Schmidt's model did, however, exert a seminal influence upon later thinkers. The well-known Paul Hersey and Kenneth Blanchard model of Situational Leadership, which identified four decision-making styles and suggested that such factors as the 'maturity' and knowledge of the group should be taken into account in choosing the appropriate style, was clearly a re-packaging of the Tannenbaum and Schmidt model.[2]

Hersey and Blanchard's Situational Leadership, like Fiedler's Contingency Theory, seems to be fading in popularity. For a time it was the market-leader in the packaged leadership training field in America and in those parts of the world most influenced by American management ideas. It is still sometimes used in conjunction with ACL. But I think that if the Tannenbaum and Schmidt model is properly taught in conjunction with the three-circles, there is really no need to introduce Hersey and Blanchard's model.

In Britain the Tannenbaum and Schmidt continuum was the subject of academic research which has greatly enhanced its standing. It is now clear that people do expect leaders to be *consistent* in personality and character (for integrity suggests loyalty to standards outside oneself), yet *flexible* when it comes to decision-making. So that an effective leader, it has been shown, will make decisions on different points of the continuum during a single working day and be right each time. For he or she will be taking into account — consciously or subconsciously — such factors as the knowledge, motivation and experience of the group or individual concerned, the time available, whether or not issues of life-and-death are involved, and the values of the particular organization. No leader or manager gets it right every time, but training can help to cut down dramatically the number of times that inappropriate choices on the decision-making continuum are made.

CONCLUSION

This brief survey of what I have called the ACL general theory in the context of developments over nearly thirty years supports the broad conclusion that it does have a unity; it is a whole which is more than a sum of its parts. Research has served to buttress the outline framework that was assembled — often intuitively — in the early days of ACL.

For these reasons ACL general theory will continue to be of use in the future. Eventually, no doubt, someone will advance a new general theory to replace it, one that proves to be of equal or better worth as the basis for selecting, training and developing leaders. But until that day comes we cannot afford to pension it off.

3 The Fifty-Fifty Rule

No man does anything from a single motive.
Samuel Taylor Coleridge

You may probably have come across the Pareto Principle in your study of management. The Pareto Principle, named after an Italian economist, states that the significant items of a given group form a relatively small part of the total. For example, twenty per cent of the sales force will bring in eighty per cent of the business. As that ratio seems to hold true in many areas, it is often called the eighty/twenty rule or the concept of 'the vital few and trivial many'. I came across it in the context of time management: eighty per cent of your really productive and creative work will be done in twenty per cent of your time.

It occurred to me that a similar principle is at work in the field of motivation, which could be formulated thus:

Fifty per cent of motivation comes from within a person and fifty per cent from his or her environment, especially from the leadership encountered there.

The Fifty-Fifty Rule in motivation does not claim to identify the different proportions in the equation exactly. It is more like a rough-and-ready rule of thumb. In effect it says no more than that a substantial part of motivation lies within a person while a substantial part lies, so to speak, outside and beyond their control.

A child, for example, might have a potential interest in science and be generally ambitious to do well at school and go to university. But the Fifty-Fifty Rule comes into play. Fifty per cent of the child's progress will depend upon the academic quality of the school and in particular upon the personality and ability of the science teacher. A great schoolteacher has been defined as 'one whose actual lessons may be forgotten, but whose living enthusiasm is a quickening, animating and inspiring power'.[1]

The Fifty-Fifty Rule does have the benefit of reminding leaders that they have a key part to play — for good or ill — in the motivation of people at work. Fortunately (or unfortunately) not all the cards are in their hands, for they are dealing with people who are self-motivating in various degrees. The art of leadership is to work with the natural grain of the particular wood of humanity which comes to hand. Selection is important, for — in the blunt words of the Spanish proverb — 'You cannot carve rotten wood.'

I have set out the Fifty-Fifty Rule early in this book because you should bear it in mind when reading the theories of Maslow and Herzberg on motivation. Both of these men were professors of psychology in universities and both subscribed to an exceptionally individualistic philosophy. It is not too much of an exaggeration to say that their principle would be that ninety per cent of motivation lies within the individual. Herzberg might have added that the environment and the supervision within it (he never used the word leadership) has power to *demotivate* or dissatisfy people, but he accorded managers no power to *motivate* them.

According to the ACL general theory, however, and the Fifty-Fifty Rule, both Maslow and Herzberg were overstating the case. Apart from our individual needs there are other needs emanating from the common task and the group or organization involved which have at least a potential motivational influence upon us. The value, worthwhileness or importance of the work we are doing, in the context of a changing and challenging environment, can enlist our deepest interest and engage our purposive energy. Leaders are often interpreters to us of the hidden values, needs and challenges of our daily work.

Contrary to the general tenor of Maslow and Herzberg, then, fifty per cent of our motivation lies without us. That does not, of course, mean that it is pointless to study the work of these two thinkers. Their contribution lies in the two sketch maps they have given us of the *internal* needs and motivations that individuals bring with them into the working situation, and which are to some extent or other met by work.

Before Maslow and Herzberg it was of course known that individuals have needs which connect with motives. But what these two American thinkers contributed were sketchmaps of how these needs relate to one another. Maslow's sketchmap is more general and more original. Herzberg's sketchmap, however, has the merit of applying Maslow's thought to the industrial situation. Herzberg's dichotomy of human needs into satisfiers and dissatisfiers, or motivational and hygiene factors, has — as we shall see — some validity. But its chief merit is as a teaching device: if things are presented to us in terms of black-or-white even the most purblind will notice the difference, while a presentation in terms of various shades of grey may make little impact.

There is also a valuable teaching element in the Fifty-Fifty Rule. You may recall the old proverb, 'There are no bad soldiers, only bad officers.' Now as a statement this is not really true. There *are* bad soldiers. But it's a very good maxim to teach young officers, for it puts them on their mettle. It invites them to examine themselves and their own leadership before blaming the troops. Thus it inoculates them against one form of rationalization.

'Mutiny, Sir! Mutiny in my ship!' exclaimed Nelson's friend Admiral Collingwood when told that the complaints of some men amounted to mutiny. 'If it can have arrived at that, it must be my fault and the fault of every one of my officers.'

The same maxim applies to young or older managers. If there is an industrial strike how many chief executives and managers would begin like Collingwood by blaming themselves and questioning their collective leadership? 'If you are not part of the solution you are part of the problem.' The Fifty-Fifty Rule is an invitation to get your part in the motivational relationship right.

Doubtless, like the Pareto Principle, other applications of Fifty-Fifty Rule will soon be discovered. As I have already mentioned in *Effective Teambuilding* (1986), it applies to the relative values of leadership and teamwork: fifty per cent of success depends on the team and fifty per cent on the leader. Again these are not scientific proportions. But they do indicate just how substantial is each contribution, regardless of that made by the other party. Here the Fifty-Fifty Rule challenges the leader (or team or individual team member) to get his or her part right first before criticizing the quality or contribution of the other party. It is the ultimate cure to the 'Us and Them' disease of organizations.

We could apply the same principle to the Nature versus Nurture debate. About half our destiny depends upon inherited characteristics or tendencies; the other half depends upon what we (or others) make of them. In the second part of that proposition lies the real challenge to parents and teachers. Certainly that applies in the leadership field. The idea that leaders are born and not made is a half-truth. The full truth is that they are (about) half born and (more-or-less) half made — by experience and thought, by training and practice. This mixture of self-teaching and teaching by others of course takes a lifetime. For paradoxically it takes a long time to become a natural leader.

The Fifty-Fifty Rule ties in well with the meaning of the word *motivation*. In fact it is a relatively new word, being introduced from America in the 1940s. Like the native English word *motive* it can be used as a neutral explanation of cause: what *motivated* him to commit the murder? Or it can indicate a conscious desire or to inculcate a desire for something or other: students *motivated* to learn by the encouragement of a good teacher.

The main American dictionary defines motivation in this second sense rather inaccurately as 'to provide with a motive', for the elements of motive energy can be there already. Motivation is closer in meaning to the older English concept of *motivity*: the power of initiating or producing movement. All these words — motive, motivation, motivity — come from the Latin verb 'to move'. What moves us to action may come from within or from without, or — more commonly — from some combination of inner impulse or proclivity on the one hand and outer situations or stimuli on the other.

The merit, then, of *motivation* as a word is that it fits perfectly the Fifty-Fifty Rule. For it covers both what happens inside an individual in terms of wanting to do something and also what happens outside them as they are influenced by others or by circumstances. When someone is motivating you, he or she is consciously or unconsciously seeking to change the strength and/or direction of your motive energy.

This second aspect of motivation does raise an ethical issue. As I have suggested above, we are actually dependent in varying degrees upon outside stimulation of various kinds in all aspects of our mental life, not least our motivation. But this human dependency on others can be used for our own ends. How does legitimate influence differ from manipulation?

To manipulate someone means to control or play upon them by artful, unfair or insidious means, especially to one's own advantage. Therefore there are two aspects of manipulation: the means and the ends. If it is *your* purpose and not a *common* purpose that is being served, you are running into the danger of manipulation. If the means you employ to motivate others are hidden from them or seek to bypass their conscious minds, then one is becoming a manipulator rather than a motivator.

Motivating others, therefore, should not be confused with manipulatory practices used by strong personalities to dominate weaker ones. Leadership exists in its most natural form among equals. It is not the same as domination or the exercise of power. True leaders respect the integrity of others. Bosses demand respect; leaders give respect. Granted such a relationship, based upon mutual trust and supported by a common sense of justice or fairness, then it is part of the responsibility of leaders to stir up enthusiasm for the common task.

PART TWO
Maslow and Herzberg

4 Maslow's Hierarchy of Needs

All that we do is done with an eye to something else.

Aristotle

Abraham Maslow died in 1970, having spent most of his long working life as lecturer and professor in psychology at Brandeis University in the State of New York. From an intellectual standpoint, Maslow's most formative years were those which he had spent in the late 1930s in New York, then, as he later declared, 'beyond a doubt, the centre of the psychological universe of that time.'[1] His preceding studies at the University of Wisconsin had included comparative and experimental psychology, biology and neurophysiology. In New York he concentrated upon the study of psycho-analysis under Erich Fromm, and he was himself analyzed by Emil Oberholzer, which he judged to be 'the best learning experience of all'. But discussions with Alfred Adler not only introduced him to some of the shortcomings of the various forms of the Freudian theory, but also gave him a lasting sense that Adler's own contribution had been insufficiently appreciated by American psychologists.

Besides the analytical school, Maslow also studied the two other incipient schools in the contemporary psychology of his day, which he named respectively the 'holistic' and the 'cultural'. The word 'holism' (from the Greek word for whole) had been first introduced in 1926 by J. C. Smuts in his seminal book *Holism and Evolution* to describe 'the principle which makes for the origin and progress of wholes in the universe'.[2] Maslow learnt the application of the holistic approach to psychology from Max Wertheimer and Kurt Koffka, both prominent members of the *Gestalt* school. Later he believed that he had found a bridge between the holistic and analytic schools in the teachings of Kurt Goldstein, whose book *The Organism*, published in 1939, in particular exerted a profound and life-long influence on Maslow.

Apart from investigating the social and cultural aspects of

psychology, primarily with the aid of the anthropologist Ruth Benedict, Maslow also made a short field study of the Northern Blackfoot Indians. In addition, he had numerous conversations with other anthropologists in New York in the 1930s, such as Margaret Mead. But a list of his nineteen publications in that decade shows that his own academic work was still experimental in orientation, and largely concerned with aspects of the behaviour of monkeys and apes. His interest in social anthropology does not appear to have gone very deep.

In 1954, Maslow (by then at Brandeis University) published a volume of articles and papers, of which all but five had been published in the preceding thirteen years, under the title *Motivation and Personality*. Maslow had planned this collection in advance to be a synthesis of the analytical, *Gestalt* and social anthropological schools, feeling that they were 'intrinsically related to each other, and that they were subaspects of a single, larger, encompassing whole'. He also hoped that together they would help to make 'more meaningful' his earlier work in experimental psychology. 'Furthermore,' he added, 'I felt they would enable me to serve better my humanistic aims.'

'A Theory of Motivation', which appears as Chapter 5 in Maslow's book and has been quite the most influential paper in the volume so far, was first published as an article in the *Psychological Review* in 1943, and it has been reprinted many times since then. The major theme of the theory was announced in the preceding chapter, which was also published as a separate article in 1943:

> 'Man is a wanting animal and rarely reaches a state of complete satisfaction except for a short time. As one desire is satisfied, another pops up to take its place. When this is satisfied, still another comes into the foreground, etc. It is characteristic of the human being throughout his whole life that he is practically always desiring something. We are faced then with the necessity of studying the relationships of all the motivations to each other and we are concomitantly faced with the necessity of giving up the motivational units in isolation if we are to achieve the broad understanding that we seek for.'

In 'A Theory of Motivation' which followed, Maslow sought to establish 'some sort of hierarchy of prepotency' in the realm of basic human needs, and to comment upon the difference this hierarchy would make to our understanding of motivation. He discussed these basic needs and their relationship to one another under five headings, which must now be considered in turn.

THE PHYSIOLOGICAL NEEDS

The concept of physiological drives has usually been taken as the starting point for motivational theory. Maslow advocated the use of the word 'need' as an alternative to 'drive', basing his case on the notion of physical homeostasis, the body's natural effort to maintain a constant normal state of the blood-stream, coupled with the finding that appetites in the sense of preferential choices of good are a fairly efficient indicator of actual deficiencies in the body. Not all physiological needs were homeostatic, for the list could be extended to include sexual desire, sleepiness, sheer activity and maternal behaviour in animals. Indeed, if a growing loss of specificity in description was acceptable, he held that it would be possible to extend the list of physiological needs very considerably.

For two reasons Maslow considered the physical needs to be unique rather than typical of the basic human needs. First, they could be regarded as relatively independent of one another and other orders of need. Secondly, in the classic cases of hunger, thirst and sex, there was a localized physical base for the need. Yet this relative uniqueness could not be equated with isolation: the physiological needs might serve as channels for all sorts of other needs as well. The man who thinks he is hungry, for example, may be looking for security rather than carbohydrates or proteins.

If a person becomes chronically short of food and water he becomes dominated by the desire to eat and to drink, and his concern for other needs tends to be swept away. Thus the physiological needs are the most prepotent of all needs. What this prepotence means precisely is that the human being who is missing everything in life in an extreme fashion will still tend to seek satisfaction for his physiological needs rather than any others. Under such temporary dominance a person's whole attitude to the future may undergo change: 'For our chronically and extremely hungry man, Utopia can be defined simply as a place where there is plenty of food. . . Such a man may fairly be said to live by bread alone.'

Supposing, however, a person has plenty of food guaranteed to him in the foreseeable future? Then, declared Maslow, another unsatisfied need emerges to dominate the organism. In other words, a satisfied want ceases to motivate. If a man has an endless supply of bread, at once other needs emerge and they supersede the physiological needs in dominating the organism. And when these in turn are satisfied, yet higher needs emerge, and so on. This is what Maslow meant by asserting that the basic human needs are organized into a hierarchy of relative prepotency.

Maslow entered an early caveat against a possible misinterpretation of his theory by advancing the hypothesis that individuals in whom a certain need had always been gratified would be the best equipped to tolerate a later frustration in that area. On the other hand, those who had been deprived would respond in a different way to eventual satisfaction than those who had been more fortunate in their younger days.

THE SAFETY NEEDS

When the physiological needs are relatively well satisfied, a new set of needs emerges centred upon the safety of the organism. Owing to the inhibition by adults of any signs of reaction to threat or danger this aspect of human behaviour is more easily observed in children, who react in a total manner to any sudden disturbance, such as being dropped, startled by loud noises, flashing lights, by rough handling, or by inadequate support.

Maslow found other indications for the need of safety in a child's preference for routine or rhythm, for a predictable and orderly world. Injustice, unfairness or lack of consistency in the parents seem to make a child feel anxious and unsafe. 'This attitude may be not so much because of the injustice *per se* or any particular pains involved; but rather because this treatment threatens to make the world look unreliable, or unsafe, or unpredictable.' The consensus of informed opinion held that children thrived best upon a *limited* permissiveness, for they need an organized or structured world. The sight of strange, unfamiliar or uncontrollable objects, illness or death can elicit fear responses in children. 'Particularly at such times, the child's frantic clinging to his parents is eloquent testimony to their role as protectors (quite apart from their roles as food givers and love givers).'

In adults we may observe expressions of the safety needs in the common desire for employment with security of tenure, pension, and insurance schemes, and the improvement of safety conditions at work. Another attempt to seek safety and stability in the world may be seen in the very common preference for familiar rather than unfamiliar things, or for the known rather than the unknown. Maslow added also the common suggestion that the appeal of religions and philosophies, which organize the universe and the men in it into some sort of coherent whole, may in part stem from this universal human need for safety and security.

Neurotic individuals may be characterized as adults who have retained their childish attitudes to the world. They perceive the world as hostile, overwhelming and threatening. Their urge towards safety or escape may take the form of a search for some strong all-powerful protector, or become a frantic effort to order the world so that no unexpected or unfamiliar dangers will ever appear. All sorts of ceremonials, rules and formulas might be employed so that every possible contingency is guarded against. Doubtless, however, Maslow would have allowed that rituals and rules could perform quite different functions for healthy or mature people.

THE SOCIAL NEEDS

If the physiological and safety needs are met, then the needs for love, affection and belongingness emerge as the dominant centre of motivation. The person concerned will feel keenly the absence of friends, wife or children; he will strive for affectionate relations with people and for 'a place in his group'.

Although Maslow distinguished between love and sex, and he showed an awareness that love needs involve both giving and receiving love, it is an important characteristic of his psychology that he generally reserved the use of the word love for close personal relationships. There is much to be said for following later practice and calling this set the 'Social Needs'.

THE ESTEEM NEEDS

This order includes both the need or desire for a high evaluation of self (self-respect or self-esteem) and for the esteem of others. Maslow divided them into two subsidiary sets:

- the desire for strength, achievement, adequacy, mastery, competence, confidence in the face of the world, independence, and freedom; and
- the desire for reputation, prestige, status, dominance, recognition, attention, importance and appreciation.

From theological discussions of *hubris* as well as from such sources as the writings of Eric Fromm, Maslow believed that 'we have been learning more and more of the dangers of basing self-esteem on the opinions of others rather than on real capacity, competence, and adequacy to the task. The most stable and therefore most healthy self-esteem is based on *deserved* respect from others rather than on external fame or celebrity and unwarranted adulation.'

THE NEED FOR SELF-ACTUALIZATION

'Even if all these needs are satisfied,' wrote Maslow, 'we may still often (if not always) expect that a new discontent and restlessness will soon develop, unless the individual is doing what he is fitted for. A musician must make music, an artist must pain, a poet must write, if he is to be ultimately at peace with himself. What a man *can* be, he *must* be. This need we may call self-actualization.

'This term, first coined by Kurt Goldstein,[1] is being used in this book in a much more specific and limited fashion. It refers to man's desire for self-fulfilment, namely, to the tendency for him to become actualized in what he is potentially. This tendency might be phrased as the desire to become more and more what one is, to become everything that one is capable of becoming. . .

'The clear emergence of these needs usually rests upon prior satisfaction of the physiological, safety, love and esteem needs.'[2]

THE DESIRES TO KNOW AND UNDERSTAND

Maslow allowed that there were two other sets of needs which found no place in the above hierarchical order, and he felt it necessary to recognize them while making it clear that at present psychologists had little to say about them. He suggested, however, that the principle of a hierarchy of prepotency might also apply in both cases, albeit in a shadowy form. In contemporary presentations of Maslow's theory of needs in management education, these two scales are usually and unfortunately omitted altogether. It should be noted also that there is some ambiguity about Maslow's language at this point. When he wrote about 'higher needs' he is sometimes referring to esteem and self-actualization; at other times, however, he has in mind the cognitive and aesthetic needs described below.

Maslow began marshalling the evidence for such desires by noting the presence of 'something like human curiosity' in monkeys and apes. 'Studies of psychologically healthy people,' he continued, 'indicate that they are, as a defining characteristic, attracted to the mysterious, to the unknown, to the chaotic, unorganized, and unexplained. This seems to be a *per se* attractiveness; these areas are in themselves and of their own right interesting. The contrasting reaction to the well-known is one of boredom.'

The gratification of the cognitive impulses is subjectively satisfying. Moreover, 'even after we know, we are impelled to know more and more minutely and microscopically on the one hand, and on the other, more and more extensively in the direction of a world philosophy, theology etc. The facts that we acquire, if they are isolated or atomistic, inevitably get theorized about, and either analyzed or organized or both. This process has been phrased by some as the search for meaning. We shall then postulate a desire to understand, to systematize, to organize, to analyze, to look for relations and meanings, to construct a system of values.' Maslow concluded with a warning against making a too sharp dichotomy between the cognitive and the conative (or basic needs) hierarchies.

THE AESTHETIC NEEDS

Maslow was convinced 'that in *some* individuals there is a truly basic aesthetic need. They get sick (in special ways) from ugliness, and are cured by beautiful surroundings; they *crave* actively, and their cravings can be satisfied *only* by beauty. It is seen almost universally in healthy children. Some evidence of such as impulse is found in every culture and in every age as far back as the cavemen.'

The conative, cognitive and aesthetic needs overlap so much that it is impossible to separate them sharply. 'The needs for order, for symmetry, for closure, for completion of the art, for system, and for structure may be indiscriminately assigned *either* to cognitive, conative, or aesthetic, or even to neurotic needs.'

COPING AND EXPRESSIVE BEHAVIOUR

Lastly, Maslow expounded a useful distinction between coping (functional striving, purposive goal seeking) and expressive behaviour which does not try to do anything: 'it is simply a reflection of the personality.' As examples of expressive or non-functional behaviour, Maslow listed 'the random movements of a healthy child, the smile on the face of a happy man even when he is alone, the springiness of the healthy man's walk, and the erectness of his carriage'. Moreover, the *style* in which a person behaves may or may not be expressive. Yet even here Maslow warned against a false dichotomy: 'It is finally necessary to stress that expressiveness of behaviour and goal-directedness of behaviour are not mutually exclusive categories. Average behaviour is usually both.' In the later years of his life, Maslow further integrated coping behaviour (activity in response to the basic, cognitive and aesthetic needs) with expressive behaviour in his development of the concept of 'Self-Actualizing Man', as will be described later in this book.

5 The Application of Maslow's Ideas in Industry

If the building of a bridge does not enrich the awareness of those who work on it, then that bridge ought not to be built.
Franz Fanon in 'The Wretched of the Earth' (1961)

Maslow spent his working life as an academic psychologist. The relatively slight impact that his theory of a hierarchy of needs made upon other academic psychologists and psychiatrists can be explained partly by the internal state of those disciplines in the period of Maslow's lifetime, dominated as they have been by the Freudian and behaviourist orthodoxies. Among those psychologists who have specifically investigated human motivation in work, some have dismissed the theory simply as an unfounded hypothesis, while others have given it a guarded acceptance. There is some measure of agreement that the lower needs (physiological, safety and social) are organized into a hierarchy of prepotence, but less agreement that their satisfaction necessarily leads on to the experience of esteem and self-actualization needs.[1]

It is true that Maslow did occasionally make it clear that he did not regard progression up the hierarchy by means of satisfaction as an inevitable or inexorable process, but he did give the general impression that this was his underlying assumption about human nature, all things being equal. Yet it would be extremely hard, for example, to demonstrate any inherent progression from the esteem needs to the need for self-actualization. But apart from these doubts about the connections between lower and higher needs, those academic psychologists and psychiatrists who have read Maslow have received this theory with cautious but unmistakable interest as a stimulating if puzzling contribution to our knowledge of man.

DOUGLAS McGREGOR'S THEORY X AND THEORY Y

This very slow growth of interest in the academic world must be contrasted with the rapid dissemination of Maslow's ideas in industry. The person mainly responsible for this work of popularization was the late Professor Douglas McGregor. Born in Detroit in 1906, the son of a Presbyterian minister, McGregor graduated at Wayne University and worked as a social psychologist at Harvard University before becoming a professor at the Massachusetts Institute of Technology. As a management consultant he worked with Standard Oil of New Jersey, Bell Telephone, Union Carbide and Imperial Chemical Industries (UK). He had a spell of six years as President of Antioch College in Ohio but returned to MIT. He was killed in a car accident in 1962.

Two years before his death, McGregor published his most influential book, *The Human Side of Enterprise*. In the early chapters he demonstrated with considerable clarity that the assumptions which managers make about human behaviour and human nature have a profound effect upon the way they seek to manage. Apart from his readable style, unusually free from jargon, McGregor's clarity stemmed from the fact that he polarized these assumptions into two clusters of propositions or theses about human nature, which he called Theory X and Theory Y.[2] Leaving out his explanatory glosses, we can set them out as follows:

Theory X: The Traditional View of Direction and Control

(1) The average human being has an inherent dislike of work and will avoid it if he can.

(2) Because of this human characteristic dislike of work, most people must be coerced, controlled, directed, threatened with punishment to get them to put forth adequate effort toward the achievement of organizational objectives.

(3) The average human being prefers to be directed, wishes to avoid responsibility, has relatively little ambition, and wants security above all.

Theory Y: The Integration of Individual and Organizational Goals

(1) The expenditure of physical and mental effort in work is as natural as play or rest.
(2) External control and the threat of punishment are not the only means for bringing about effort toward organizational objectives. Man will exercise self-direction and self-control in the service of objectives to which he is committed.
(3) Commitment to objectives is a function of the rewards associated with their achievement.
(4) The average human being learns, under proper conditions, not only to accept but to seek responsibility.
(5) The capacity to exercise a relatively high degree of imagination, ingenuity, and creativity in the solution of organizational problems is widely, not narrowly, distributed in the population.
(6) Under the conditions of modern industrial life, the intellectual potentialities of the average human being are only partially utilized.

Now McGregor has drawn heavily upon the work of Maslow: indeed, if one subtracts the Maslow-inspired passages there is not much left of Theory Y. McGregor had swallowed Maslow's theory of a hierarchy of needs hook, line and sinker, but he digested it into language which industrial and commercial managers could understand. Moreover, he integrated the theory with the more traditional preoccupations of management by suggesting that the needs of the individual and the needs of the organization were not inherently incompatible. Under the third proposition above in the Theory Y cluster, for example, McGregor commented: 'The most significant of such rewards, e.g. the satisfaction of ego and self-actualization needs, can be direct products of efforts directed towards organizational needs.'

If Theory Y rested upon optimistic assumptions about man buttressed by the writings of Maslow, Theory X, by contrast, had a darker foundation. In company with many other behavioural scientists before and since McGregor advanced for the justification of Theory X what could be called a modern management myth about the Genesis myth. The deepest roots of Theory X go down to the Garden of Eden. 'The punishment of Adam and Eve for eating the fruit of the Tree of Knowledge was to be banished from Eden into a world where they had to work for a living.' Obviously, McGregor supposed that this myth lay behind the assumption that man has an inherent tendency to avoid work. Without doubting that pessimistic views of man both exist and exert influence upon human relationships, we may legitimately question how far these can be blamed upon such external sources as the Book of Genesis.

THE WIDER DISSEMINATION OF MASLOW'S IDEAS

McGregor's writings, still ranked as the most influential of their *genre* in the world of industry, and his persuasive lectures were not the only means by which Maslow's views have been propagated to management audiences. His disciples included such prominent behavioural scientists as Rensis Likert and Chris Argyris. Likert, as Director of Institute for Social Research at Michigan University, studied the effects of different supervisors on the productivity of those who work under them, and found a significant correlation between high production and supervision which helped operatives to do the job well for their own satisfaction as much as for the attainment of departmental goals.[3] Argyris, as Professor of Industrial Administration at Yale University, tended to stress the element of conflict between the individual's and the organization's respective needs for self-actualization, but he added his powerful voice to the chorus advocating practical steps — such as 'job enlargement' and participation in problem solving and decision-making — for reconciling the two sets of goals.[4]

Maslow's theory also attracted the attention of sociologists as well as social psychologists. For example, in a study of the attitudes to work of 229 manual workers in Luton factories (Vauxhall, Skefko Ball Bearings, and Laporte Chemicals) J. H. Goldthorpe and his colleagues accepted that attempts to specify the range and structure of a hierarchy of human needs along the lines of Maslow might be both legitimate and relevant, but they expressed doubts as to whether or not one could make easy deductions about these general statements to particular cases.

There were particular sociological factors behind what they called the Luton workers' largely 'instrumental' attitude to their work — looking upon it as an instrument or means towards relatively high wages. 'For wants and expectations are culturally determined *variables*, not psychological constants; and from a sociological standpoint what is in fact of major interest *is* the variation in the ways in which groups differently located in the social structure actually experience and attempt to meet the needs which at a different level of analysis may be attributed to them all.'[5] To social factors we must add such personal variables as parental upbringing.[6] Moreover, where people are in their life-cycle has some influence on what needs are dominant in their experience as motivating forces.

Goldthorpe's conclusion matched that of John Mason Brown. Writing in *Esquire* (April, 1960) he said: 'Most people spend most of their days doing what they do not want to do in order to earn the right, at times, to do what they may desire.'

THE MORAL ISSUE

For at least some sociologists the discrepancy between Maslow's description of human nature and the lack of desire for self-actualization in some working environments has raised a moral issue. What place *ought* work to occupy in human life, quite apart from the role it may play in such loaded settings as the Luton factories? What changes — if any — in the social and cultural *milieu* should be encouraged, and why? The British industrial sociologist Alan Fox posed the issue in the following way:

> 'The broadest division is between those doctrines which seek to persuade us that work ought to be a central integrating principle of man's individual and social being, offering opportunities of choice, decision, and responsibility, and those who find no ethical difficulty in seeing its major significance in terms of its extrinsic outcome.'[7]

Thus the application of Maslow's theory of a hierarchy of human needs to the task of understanding attitudes and behaviour at work in industry has already raised some fundamental moral questions about the place of work in life. But this is a secondary debate, albeit an important one. For even those who reject the liberal demand that work should now be so arranged as to allow maximum satisfaction possible in all five areas of individual need would accept that work should provide at least the financial means for pursuing the all-important goal of self-actualization outside the factory or the office, namely in leisure activities and family life. Either way the psychology of self-fulfilment as exemplified by Maslow's theory of needs marches on.

Later I shall subject the concept of self-actualization in the thought of Maslow to a much closer scrutiny, because there are some important differences between his actual views on that subject and some popular versions of that philosophy. In particular his later teaching on how self-actualization can and cannot be achieved needs to be grasped, for this differs in some respects from his earlier and tentative suggestion of a necessary or causal link with the satisfaction of lower needs, as implied in the theory above.

Next, however, in the following two chapters I shall consider the theory, researches and assumptions of Frederick Herzberg. There are two main reasons for doing so. The first reason is that Herzberg has both offered what purports to be an alternative theory to that of Maslow and has also claimed that evidence gathered by empirical methods proves his theory to be true. A second reason is that it keeps us in touch with the practical concerns of industry. For Herzberg was a leading exponent of that school which holds that work should play a central and integral (rather than instrumental) part in the process of healthy self-actualization, not simply for the few but for the masses employed in industry.

6 Herzberg's Motivation-Hygiene Theory

Work is not the curse, but drudgery is.
Henry Ward Beecher

In 1959 Frederick Herzberg published his research into job attitudes in a book entitled *The Motivation to Work*. At the time of writing Herzberg, later Professor of Psychology at Western Reserve University, was Research Director at the Psychological Service of Pittsburgh. His co-authors, Bernard Mausner and Barbara Snyderman, were respectively Research Psychologist and Research Associate at the same institute.

With two other psychologists Herzberg and Mausner had carried out an earlier preliminary survey of the existing literature on the factors involved in attitudes to work.[1] Despite differences in content and methods in the 155 books and articles they considered, Herzberg and his colleagues felt able to draw a major conclusion:

> 'The one dramatic finding that emerged in our review of this literature was the fact that there was a difference in the primacy of factors, depending upon whether the investigator was looking for things the worker liked about his job or things he disliked. The concept that there were some factors that were 'satisfiers' and others that were 'dissatisfiers' was suggested by this finding. From it was derived one of the basic hypotheses of our own study.'

BASIC CHARACTERISTICS OF THE RESEARCH PROJECT

After two pilot schemes, involving respectively thirteen labourers, clerical workers, foremen, plant engineers and accountants, and thirty nine middle-managers (all but six of them engineers of one kind or another), the research team launched into a study of the job attitudes of 203 engineers and accountants working in nine factories or plants around Pittsburgh. The description and discussion of this particular research project formed the main content of *The Motivation to Work*; moreover, the methodology of the research served as a model for many replications in the next decade. Consequently it is important to grasp the essential methodological characteristics of the research Herzberg and his colleagues undertook. Owing to the style of the writers this is not always an easy task, but we can distinguish three major characteristics:

1. *Specification of Experience*

Each of the 203 subjects was asked to identify periods in his own history when his feelings about his job were markedly either higher or lower than usual. The researcher made the assumption that the respondents would be able to recognize the extremes of this continuum of feelings and to select extreme situations to report. They distinguished between short and long-term sequences of events, but in each case the 'story' had to be finite in terms of having a beginning, middle and end.

2. *Factors-Attitudes-Effects*

The research aimed at unravelling the inter-relations between objective 'events' in the historical accounts, coupled with the feelings which were expressed about them by the subjects, and the effects which resulted. Rather confusingly, the reported events were labelled 'first-level factors' and the allied feelings 'second-level factors', while the word 'factor' was also used about the combination of both together. The word 'attitude' means in this context the more settled or habitual mode of regarding aspects of life. 'Effects' included job performance (based on the subject's own reports of quantifiable or qualitative changes), mental health, inter-personal relationships, attitude towards the company and other attitudes allied to the working situation.

3. *Research Methods*

The researchers employed the technique of the 'semi-structured' interview, in which the interviewer asks some pre-arranged questions but has freedom to pursue any lines of inquiry that he judges might be fruitful. 'The questions were so designed that for each story we were sure to get the factors-attitudes-effects information for which we sought.' Each respondent could choose a story about a time when he felt exceptionally good or exceptionally bad about the job. After this sequence had been thoroughly discussed and analyzed, the interviewer asked for a second story, which had to be opposite in terms of good/bad and short/long range sequence of events from the first one. Some respondents volunteered a third or fourth story.

The researchers attempted to set up categories of factors and effects from the material gathered. Carefully cross-checking one another's judgements, the team broke down the replies into 'thought units', which was defined as 'a statement about a single event or condition that led to a feeling, a single characterization of a feeling, or a description of a single effect', e.g. the statement 'The way it was given to me showed the supervisor had confidence in my work.' A sample of 5,000 'thought units'; of the entire (unspecified) total was sorted out into three major categories: first-level factors, second-level factors and effects. Each of these main ones was further sub-divided into lesser categories. Once ninety five per cent agreement among them on the categories had been achieved, the research team proceeded to analyze 476 stories or 'sequences of events'.

THE CATEGORIES

Under the heading of 'First-Level Factors' the authors listed fourteen categories of elements or acts in the situation which the respondents found to be sources of good or bad feelings, with the criteria which they had used to establish them.

1. *Recognition.* Any act of recognition, be it notice, praise or criticism ('negative recognition') served as the main criterion. The sub-categories allowed distinction between situations when concrete rewards were given along with the acts of recognition and those in which they were not.

2. *Achievement.* Stories mentioning some specific success (or failure) were placed in this category, e.g. successful completion of a job, solutions to problems, vindication, and seeing the results of one's work.

3. *Possibility of Growth*. Respondents mentioned changes in their situations involving objective evidence that the possibilities for professional growth had increased or decreased. Besides new vistas opened up by promotion this category included reports of increased opportunities in the existing situation for learning and practising new skills, or acquiring new professional knowledge.

4. *Advancement*. 'This category was used only when there was an actual change in the status or position of the person in the company.'

5. *Salary*. 'This category included all sequences of events in which compensation plays a role. Surprisingly enough, virtually all of these involve wage or salary increases, or unfulfilled expectation of salary increases.'

6. *Inter-personal relations*. Under this general heading actual verbalizations about the characteristics of the interaction between the respondent and some other individual were divided into three categories according to the identity of the latter: superior, subordinate and peers. These were interactions which might take place in working hours but were independent of the activities of the job.

7. *Supervision-technical*. This category included remarks about the competence or incompetence, fairness, or unfairness of the supervisor or superior. Comments upon the superior's willingness to delegate or teach, on his tendency to nag or perpetually criticize, would be classified under 'supervision-technical'.

8. *Responsibility*. This category covered those sequences of events in which the respondent mentioned satisfaction gained from being given (or denied) responsibility. 'In cases, however, in which the story revolved around a wide gap between a person's authority and the authority he needed to carry out his job responsibilities the factor identified was "company policy and administration". The rationale for this was that such a discrepancy between authority and job responsibilities would be considered evidence of poor management.'.

9. *Company policy and administration*. This category included descriptions of adequate or inadequate organization and management. Apart from such structural components remarks about the over-all characteristics of the company's policy (especially its personnel policy) as harmful or beneficial were placed under this heading.

10. *Working conditions*. Comments about the physical con-

ditions of work, the amount of work, facilities available, ventilation, tools, space and other environmental aspects came into this class of 'thought units'.

11. *Work itself*. Mentions of the actual doing of the job, or phases of it, as sources of satisfaction or dissatisfaction found places in this category.

12. *Factors in personal life*. This factor covered a range of statements about cases in which work impinged upon personal life in such a way that the effect was an ingredient in the respondent's feelings about his job. Family needs for salary levels or problems stemming from job location would be examples of this type of comment.

13. *Status*. This term was employed to classify any actual mentions of signs or appurtenances of status as being constituents in reaction to the job, e.g. a secretary, company car, a certain eating facility.

14. *Job security*. Objective signs of the presence or absence of job security, such as tenure and company stability or instability, were listed under this factor.

Under the heading of 'Second Level Factors' the researchers analyzed the responses of the interviewee to the question, 'What did these events mean to you?' Naturally the information at this point was limited by the extent to which the respondents could articulate their feelings and the level of insight which enabled them to report real perceptions rather than stereotyped reactions based on socially accepted ideas. These second-level inferences or generalizations were therefore to be distinguished from the statements of feeling in the verbal responses of the 'first-level' factors. The eleven second-level factors or clusters of feelings share for the most part the same names as the first-level ones; for example: recognition, achievement, possible growth, responsibility, belonging and interest. 'Feelings about salary' was included to cover those situations in which 'the first-level factor was viewed primarily as a source of the things that money can bring. If an answer to the question, "Why did this promotion make you feel good?" was, "I like the idea of being able to make more money", then the second-level factor was coded "salary ".'

The analysis of *effects* into categories posed fewer problems, because most respondents were specific and concrete in their replies.

1. *Performance effects*. This major category included three sub-

categories. The first consisted of general comments about work being better or worse than usual; the second embraced comments about the rate of work; and in the third were mustered remarks concerning the quality of work.

2. *Turnover*. At one end of the 'turnover' continuum the respondent actually resigned or left his job; at the other his positive feelings about his work and the company had mounted so considerably that he turned down attractive offers to go elsewhere.

3. *Mental health effects*. Positive statements included a lessening of tension symptoms, gaining weight when underweight, and stopping too much drinking or smoking. The more numerous negative reports, however, mentioned psychomatic effects (skin disorders, ulcers, heart conditions), physiological changes related to tensions (such as severe headaches and loss of appetite), and more diffuse symptoms of anxiety possibly related to temperamental dispositions in the individual.

4. *Effects on inter-personal relationships*. There were many instances where the job had appeared to influence for better or worse a man's relationships with his family.

5. *Additional effects*. Respondents also reported changed attitudes towards themselves, their colleagues, their professions or the companies which employed them.

EXPERIMENTAL RESULTS

The major question that the research team had posed themselves was whether or not different kinds of factors brought about job satisfaction and job dissatisfaction. A number of minor questions which interested them related to the correlations between the variables of long-term and short-term sequences, first-level and second-level factors, effects and attitudes, profession, education, job level and experience. Broadly speaking, the team felt convinced that their main hypothesis that there *were* two distinct sets of factors involved had been justified by the study. 'The factors that are rarely instrumental in bringing about high job attitudes focus not on the job itself but rather on the characteristics of the context in which the job is done: working conditions, inter-personal relationships, supervision, company policies, administration of these policies, effects on the worker's personal life, job security, and salary. This is a basic distinction. The satisfiers relate to the *actual job*. Those factors that do not act as satisfiers describe the *job situation*.'

Heading the list of short-term 'satisfiers' in the first-level factors are *achievement* and *recognition*, followed by *work itself, responsibility, advancement* and the *possibility of growth*. In the second-level area the *possibility of growth* appeared with great frequency in the 'high satisfaction' stories. By reviewing all the variables the team suggested that the complex or cluster of achievement - recognition - responsibility - work itself - advancement are highly interrelated in both the short and long terms. 'When some or all of the factors are present in the job situation of an individual, the fulfilment of his basic needs is such that he enters a period of exceptionally positive feelings about his job.' For situational, professional or personal reasons the relative strengths of factors may vary, but the complex as a whole will always characterize job satisfaction.

Visually the discontinuity between the 'satisfiers' and 'dissatisfiers' and their relative longevity can be shown by means of a diagram. 'As indicated in the legend of this figure, the distance from the neutral area shows the percentage frequency with which each factor occurred in the high job-attitude sequences and in the low job-attitude sequences. The width of the boxes represents the ratio of long-range to short-range attitude effects; the wider the box, the more frequently this factor led to a long-range job attitude change. The factors of recognition and achievement are shaded in this figure to indicate that the width of their boxes portrays a reversal in the long-range ratio. The attitude effects of both of these factors were substantially more short range.'

The frequency and duration of *work itself, responsibility* and *advancement* suggest that they form the major strands of high job attitudes. They appear much less frequently in stories of times when the respondents felt unhappy with their job. These motivating factors focussed on the job itself; the 'dissatisfiers' are concerned with the context of environment of the job. Salary has a short-term satisfying effect, but as an influence on job attitudes the research team concluded that it had more potency as a dissatisfier than as a satisfier. In the 'low' stories money tended to reflect a perceived unfairness in the wages policy or system of the company; in the 'high' stories it accompanied achievement: 'it meant more than money; it meant a job well done; it meant that the individual was progressing in his work.'

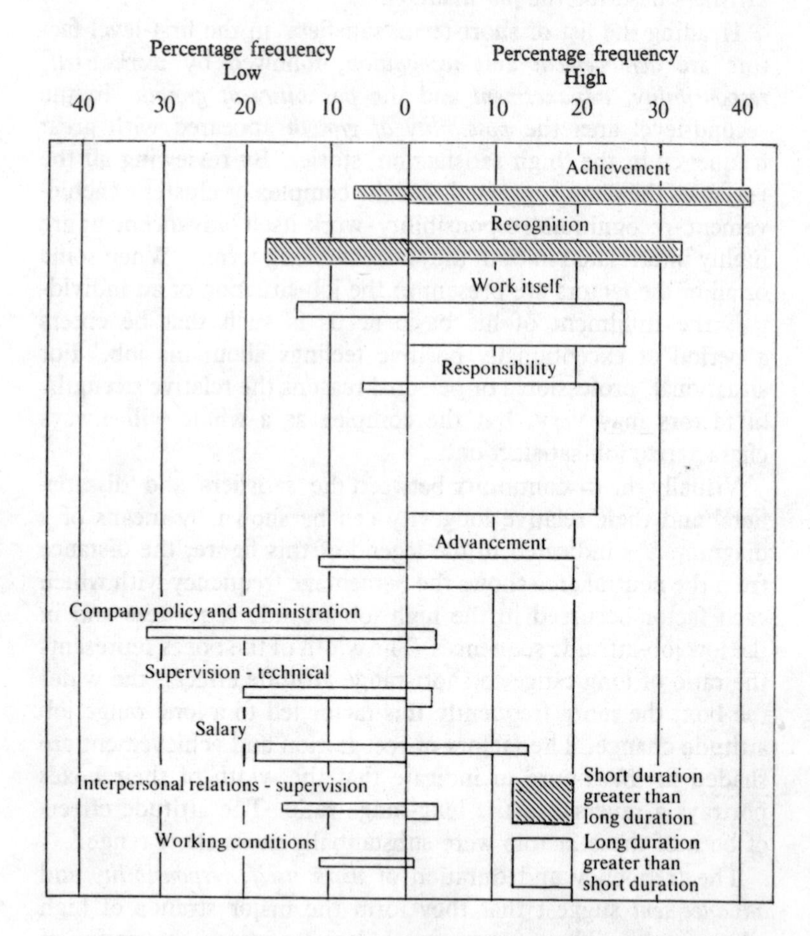

Figure 6.1 *Comparison of satisfiers and dissatisfiers (203 Pittsburgh engineers and accountants).*

From their analysis of the 'second-level' factors, Herzberg and his colleagues concluded that 'a sense of personal growth and of self-actualization is the key to an understanding of positive feelings about the job. We would define the first-level factors of achievement-responsibility-work itself-advancement as a complex of factors leading to this sense of personal growth and self-actualization. In a later discussion we postulate a basic need for these goals as a central phenomenon in understanding job attitudes.' Short-term positive feelings can then be regarded as 'partial reinforcements' of these basic needs.

For the complex of factors which describe the *surrounds* of the job and can cause discontent Herzberg recruited the word *hygiene* from the medical world. 'Hygiene operates to remove health hazards from the environment of man. It is not a curative; it is, rather, a preventive. Modern garbage disposal, water purification, and air-pollution do not cure diseases, but without them we would have more diseases.'[5] The 'satisfier' Herzberg and his associates named *motivators*. The former they linked with the 'avoidance needs', or the human tendency to avoid painful or unpleasant situations; the latter they connected directly with the concept that man's 'ultimate goal' is self-actualization or self-realization. In the work situation this general basic need finds a degree of fulfilment if the job allows some meeting of the related needs for professional growth and for the exercise of creativity. If these possibilities are intrinsically absent from the job, then heavy compensations in terms of hygiene factors would be necessary to adjust the balance. 'The motivators fit the need for creativity, the hygiene factors satisfy the need for fair treatment, and it is thus that the appropriate incentive must be present to achieve the desired job attitude and job performance.'

HERZBERG AND MASLOW

How does Herzberg's motivator-hygiene theory relate to Maslow's theory of a hierarchy of needs? Clearly they share in common the concept of self-actualization, derived from the writings of Jung, Adler, Sullivan, Rogers and Goldstein. Herzberg's discussion of Maslow's theory in *The Motivation to Work* is both brief and unsatisfactory. The aspect of the theory which he seems to have felt most unacceptable was the notion that the predominant needs of individuals might change and develop, rather than being seen as relatively fixed and immutable. Yet although Herzberg pressed home his distinction between the 'motivators' and 'hygiene', he himself allowed for some possibility of a fluctuating 'need hierarchy' operating within the two clusters, just as he left open the question as to whether different degrees of potency among the factors in the two sets would reflect different patterns of psychological characteristics in professional groups or individuals.

In contrast to the predominantly holistic bias of Maslow's mind, Herzberg's approach exhibits a dichotomizing tendency towards either/or and black-or-white thinking. It is possible that the opposite ends or poles of continuums in human behaviour may appear to take on a qualitative difference. By documenting such a phenomenon in relation to work Herzberg indirectly drew attention to the differing characteristics of Maslow's 'basic needs'. Physiological, safety and social needs, for example, might create dissatisfaction if they were not met, but they had little power to afford satisfaction. By contrast, the meeting of esteem and self-actualization needs could lead to a more positive and longer-lasting sense of satisfaction. On the other hand, the absence of a potential for self-actualizing progress might not create conscious dissatisfaction. Thus it could be said that Herzberg was only developing the hint in Maslow that the physiological needs form a poor model for the 'higher' needs in the hierarchy.[2] Moreover, Herzberg accepted the possibility, pending further research, that an individual's internal rating of 'satisfiers' and 'dissatisfiers' might reflect his personality development, i.e. presumably his progress in gratifying the hierarchy of basic needs. It is clear also that some psychologists (like some theologians and philosophers) have a temperamental bias towards dichotomizing, while others have predominantly holistic or synthetic minds.[3] Herzberg belongs to the first group, Maslow to the second. Allowing for the application to the work situation in particular and also the respective intellectual biases of the two psychologists, it may be concluded that the similarities between the approaches of Maslow and Herzberg outweigh their dissimilarities.[4]

CONFIRMATIONS

In *The Motivation to Work* Herzberg and his colleagues recognized that they were making an inference when arguing from the particular (203 Pittsburgh engineers and accountants) to the general, but they felt that the 'lack of individual differences in the occurrence of factors and effects argues the applicability of our findings beyond the immediate bounds of the small sample with which we worked.' They predicted that similar studies of a broader spectrum of educational and occupational backgrounds would reveal wider differences than they had found by comparing engineers with accountants. They expected less 'satisfiers' to be uncovered by research on routine assembly-line workers, for example, but the quality of the unhappy work experiences would probably vary little according to type of job or educational level.

In *Work and the Nature of Man* (1963), Herzberg could report the completion of some seventeen replications of the initial work, using the same research methodology but under the direction of other investigators, which included studies of the following occupations:

Finn Supervisors
Women in the Professions
Hospital Nurses
Scientists
Manufacturing Supervisors
Female Assemblers
Unskilled Hospital Employees
Hungarian Engineers
Technicians

Herzberg concluded that these studies verified his 'Motivation-Hygiene Theory'. Any discrepancies between them and the Pittsburgh findings could be explained away. For example, the fact that *salary* was mentioned only once as a significant dissatisfier and as often as not appeared as a satisfier led to a justification for Herzberg's early view that money belonged primarily to 'hygiene', or the context of the job, along the following lines. First, the negative effect of salary when coupled with a dissatisfaction event endures much longer than the positive results when it is associated with a satisfaction event. Secondly, Herzberg reiterated the conclusion that negatively money always reflected discontent with other hygiene factors, and positively it accompanied or marked advancement. A third cultural reason could be advanced: 'All hygiene needs are connected with salary and, because of this, *salary* is the most visible, communicable and advertised factor in all the world of work. *Salary* permeates the thoughts and expressions of people when they view their jobs. In such a circumstance, it is hardly surprising that *salary* often seems to be a satisfier to the individual. If so many hygiene needs can be fulfilled by money, then it is difficult not to conceive of it as a source of happiness.'

Herzberg's treatment of another 'inversion', as he called the phenomenon of a 'motivator' being reported as a 'dissatisfier' and *vice versa*, raises more serious questions. Three of the seventeen groups studied found positive satisfaction in the *inter-personal relationships* on the job. The first, a group of lower-level supervisors in utility companies, reported that getting along with their subordinates made them more happy than failure to get along with them made them unhappy. Herzberg interpreted this finding in relation to their level of management and the kind of organizations in which they worked as evidence of 'a kind of pathology or sickness in their motivational pattern'.

Herzberg's general view that 'supervision' (he never called it leadership) is a hygiene factor obstinately ignores the fact that in many circumstances human relationships are as much intrinsic to the job as they are extrinsic. His attempt to distinguish between *inter-personal relationships* and *supervision-technical* does not alter his under-estimation of the satisfying or motivating influence of good leadership, both for the leader himself or herself and for those working with him or her.

Herzberg appears to have a curiously rigid idea about management. The idea that leaders at all levels might be aware and respond to the needs of those working under them does not seem to have occurred to him at all. A stress on the vital importance of good leadership to ensure achievement and recognition, the delegation of responsibility and the provision of challenging tasks, finds no place in his writings, although he did allow that better supervision would be required if jobs were to be made more intrinsically satisfying. In other words, Herzberg may well have reacted so vigorously against the 'human relations' approach to management, personified by the growth of 'group sensitivity training', that he threw out the baby with the bath water.

This thesis may be supported by Herzberg's cavalier treatment of the two groups of professional women in government service who found some satisfaction in effective *inter-personal relationships* with their subordinates and fellow employees. In Herzberg's 'rational explanation' these innocent feelings were interpreted as 'a sickness in motivation . . . brought about by the insecurity of women competing in a traditionally masculine domain.' These comments illustrate the danger that Herzberg's dichotomy between 'satisfaction' and 'dissatisfaction', job content and job context, can become a Procrustean bed upon which all experience, suitably lopped and trimmed, must be made to fit. In fact there is considerable evidence that leadership and good human relationships contribute to both work achievement and individual job satisfaction.

Herzberg's discussion of the studies in motivation which had appeared between 1959 and 1966 illustrates his either/or thinking. Of those studies which adopted the more traditional questionnaire approach, with lists of job attitude factors to be ranked, rated or selected, Herzberg disposed of those by R. B. Ewen and by P. Wernimont and M. Dunnette on the grounds that they exhibited both semantic confusions and some methodological flaws.[5] Other researchers he felt gave general support to his theory, including one undertaken on a sample of 2,665 workers under the age of thirty employed in heavy or light industries around Leningrad,[6] deducing that 'the basic factor which imparts the greatest influence on the attitude to work is the content and character of the work itself' was as true in a Marxist as in a capitalist society.

Some studies have also given support for Herzberg's belief that his theory would illuminate motivation not only in the professional and skilled occupations but also in the lower levels of unskilled and manual work.[7] These help to mitigate the charge that Herzberg has generalized from essentially middle-class samples. Other articles have buttressed the central Herzberg thesis. For example, a study of over seven hundred employees in three large banks in the western states of America confirmed that feelings of satisfaction springing from intrinsic job factors last longer than those stemming from the work context.[8]

CRITICS OF HERZBERG'S THEORY

The hypothesis that there are exclusive sets of 'satisfiers' and 'dissatisfiers' has been denied by other empirical investigators, apart from those already mentioned. As we have seen, these writers have blurred the sharp edges of the dichotomy by showing that intrinsic factors may act as dissatisfiers and extrinsic (or contextual) factors can serve as satisfiers.[9] Industrial sociologists have confirmed this view, with suitable reservations. Alan Fox has summed up their views with the suggestion that there is a useful distinction between satisfaction *in* a job and satisfaction *with* a job.[10] Those who have attempted an impartial review of the literature in the 'Herzberg controversy' have concluded that the intrinsic-extrinsic dichotomy does not adequately reflect the sources of positive and negative attitudes to work: in short, they regard it as an over-simplification.[11]

Once the flaws in Herzberg's dichotomy between 'satisfiers' and 'dissatisfiers' became apparent, it was only a question of time before the unidimensional Maslow hierarchy would be advocated as a theoretical model for research on the shop floor.[12] In a British study of 290 female shop floor and ex-shop floor workers in electrical and electronic engineering firms it was found that thirty per cent expressed general dissatisfaction with their work. The analysis of their multi-choice questionnaires and unstructured interviews revealed the overriding importance of the work itself as a determinant of job satisfaction or dissatisfaction.[13]

R. Wild and his colleagues, however, found no evidence to support Herzberg's 'principle of duality', although the practical implications were similar. In their study, the shopfloor workers perceived their supervisors as being sources of both support and motivation. Wages, supportive supervision and personal relationships were contingent factors relating to lower level needs, and could be compared to Herzberg's maintenance (hygiene) factors. 'The distinctive difference between our satisfied and dissatisfied subjects lay in the lack of self-actualization perceived by the latter in relation to their work.' Those who experienced some degree of self-actualization found their work more interesting, varied, challenging, and allowing more opportunities for achievement and the use of abilities than those who felt frustrated. The fact that thirty per cent in the *same* job were dissatisfied confirms the thesis that individual attitudes and values inevitably produce different perceptions of work.

CONCLUSION

In retrospect, the research work of Herzberg and his colleagues, and the studies which his theory has provoked, confirm the view that work in industry and large organizations can be a means for at least the partial satisfaction of man's higher needs. Some support for Maslow's theory of prepotence is also afforded by the finding that if work does not provide adequate means for meeting the lower needs, it is experienced as positively dissatisfying, more so than if opportunities for more intrinsic satisfactions are missing. Herzberg's dualistic framework has a value as a stimulating and introductory visual sketch-map in teaching, but it becomes an over-simplication if taken beyond a certain point. Moreover, his apparent contradiction of Maslow turns out to be more a symptom of differences in casts of mind rather than anything more fundamental in theory.

Herzberg's particular contribution was his passionate concern for people, matched with an evangelistic fervour for the gospel that industrial work, as much as any other form of work, should serve the humanistic purpose of self-actualization. So much so that jobs which do not lend themselves to this end are to be 'enriched' until they do, or mechanized out of existence. In cases where mechanization or automation is impossible, 'hygiene factors', such as big financial rewards, must clearly be seen to be compensations for being sub-human.

With a new faith in man and some professional ingenuity, however, it will be possible to enrich most jobs so that they win more of both intrinsic satisfactions and extrinsic rewards for the worker. In keeping with the behavioural science school as a whole, Herzberg's public platform was that such job enrichment leads to more motivation, which in turn yields higher company profits. But these practical arguments rest upon certain philosophical foundations, which need careful testing to see if they can alone support the weight.

PART THREE | *Work and the Nature of Man*

7 The Philosophical Context in Brief

I tell you, sir, the only safeguard of order and discipline in the modern world is a standardized worker with interchangeable parts. That would solve the entire problem of management.
Jean Giraudoux, writing in 1944

As psychologists, Maslow and Herzberg based their theories upon some sort of empirical evidence, but they openly confess to holding and propagating certain philosophical assumptions about the nature of man. It is these assumptions which have entered the blood-stream of society by way of the veins of management education. The time is now ripe to evaluate these assumptions.

First, however, it is necessary to set the writings of Maslow and Herzberg in context within the field of management studies. The earliest school of management thought tended to equate work with production, and to justify the nature of jobs by the yardstick of productivity, which led to the fragmenting of functions. In 1776, Adam Smith had observed the causal relationship between specialization and productivity: 'the division of labour, however, so far as it can be introduced, occasions, in every act, a proportionate increase of the productive powers of labour.'[1] Specialization, however, which meant a decrease in the number of operations a worker performed, led inexorably to more repetitive work for the majority, a long process which culminated in the assembly line. Undoubtedly in extreme cases such work produced ill-health, and a widespread sense of meaninglessness which some nineteenth century thinkers called 'alienation'.

Whatever the philosophical or religious views of individual employers it is difficult to avoid the conclusion that industry as such during its formative years held a mechanistic view of man: he was treated as a 'hand', an interchangeable cog in the factory machine. It would be perhaps more true to say, however, that industry, intent upon increasing production, held no particular philosophy of man but only that he had contracted his necessary labour for better wages than he would earn in the fields. For the factory owner the way that labour was organized seemed to depend solely upon the task.

Before the First World War, except for relatively minor concessions to humanitarian reformers and trades union leaders in the preceding decades of the nineteenth and earlier twentieth centuries, the demands of technology reigned unchallenged. Production measured progress, and the lesser individual hardships of the working classes (always preferable to unemployment and starvation) must not interfere with the advance of civilization. As F. W. Taylor (1856–1917), the father of time-and-motion work study, could declare: 'In my judgement, the best possible measure of the height in the scale of civilization to which any people has risen is its productivity.'[2]

The researches of Elton Mayo and his associates in the Hawthorne factories of General Electric during the 1930s form a watershed in management thought, dividing us from what is sometimes known as the 'classical' school. Although the precise interpretation of these American experiments remains in some dispute, their wide and seminal influence cannot be denied.[3] As a result of them it was now held that workers should be regarded as members of an 'informal social organism' rather than as individuals; for example, as a group they could, and did, restrict output according to unwritten group standards. In other words, they apparently valued the social benefits of belonging to the group more than the financial rewards for high individual productivity, incentives which had been at the centre of the 'carrot and stick' approach to motivating the workers.

These researchers furthered the rapid growth of social psychology over the past fifty years, a process which in turn stimulated the development of the 'human relations' school of thought in management studies. In brief, this latter alliance or school of psychologists and managers propounded the view that in order to maintain and increase production it had become necessary to cater for the social needs of employees. For them the group and the quality of the 'human relations' within it took over first place as the determining factor in high production.

Such ideas, apparently backed by empirically gathered facts, also proved to be most acceptable to those who saw them as scientific evidence for the democratic values of the American way of life. Moreover, they both fostered and were fostered by the emerging ideology of the social sciences, which can be described in general terms as optimistic in terms of the perfectibility of man, liberal in manifesting a profound distaste for any form of authoritarianism, and humanist in its world-view and values.

The theories of Herzberg and the 'job enrichment' school, based upon philosophy of individual self-fulfilment exemplified by Maslow, may be seen both as a development of the 'classical' and 'human relations' schools and also as a reaction against them. If Herzberg and his colleagues shared much the same methods and justifications as the former, yet they also can claim to be as 'employee centred' as the latter. It is mainly a question of emphasis. Their third school of thought focussed almost entirely upon the needs which the individual brings with him to work, rather than upon either the needs of the task or the needs of the group in the situation.

8 Herzberg's View of Man

The noblest work of God? Man. Who found it out? Man.

Mark Twain

In the final chapter of *The Motivation to Work*, Herzberg and his colleagues posed two questions. First, how far were they justified in generalizing about human nature from a study of 203 American middle-managers? Secondly, what implications did their findings have for industry and the community today?

The discussion of the first question led the authors to take a brief, selective and somewhat distorted view of history, ranging in a few pages from the Biblical era to the Machine Age. The present century was characterized by a sense of alienation in the individual. Among the causes for this psychological rootlessness is the substitution of bureaucratic organization and control over the worker for the former authority of the master workman, which was based on skill. The authors then assert the necessity for restructuring many industrial jobs so that the individuals concerned had more control over the way in which their work was done.

MYTHS OF MAN

In *Work and the Nature of Man* (1966), as the title implied, Herzberg returned to these larger issues. It is true that most of the book is devoted to describing and discussing research studies since 1959 which Herzberg believed had confirmed the universal applicability of his motivation-hygiene theory. The first five chapters, however, deal with the wider philosophical and historical aspects of work.

In the first chapter Herzberg advances the thesis that industry is now the dominant institution of modern times. In earlier epochs the army and the Church respectively occupied that position. Now the business ethos pervades almost every sphere, including the universities. 'Perhaps the professor and his remembered institution are part of the romantic past, for he is no longer "a scholar in a community of scholars" but an employee of a large quasi-business organization merchandizing (with appropriate cultural noises) technology, and he is seeking fringe benefits just as avidly as his nonprofessional counterparts in industry proper.'

At this point Herzberg confuses what should be kept separate, namely the proper and legitimate interest of universities and churches in improving their organizational life in terms of their distinctive aims on the one hand, and the intrusion of 'the values of the market' into these areas on the other hand. The latter, the dominance of the business ethos, has often been announced in the United States. The supremacy of the business interest was proclaimed, for example, by President Calvin Coolidge with his vivid slogan: 'The business of America is business.' Clearly Herzberg has a case for asserting the dominance of industry in the fabric of social life, but he overstates it in these pages.

As signs of the new willingness of industry as the dominant institution to assume responsibility for the moral leadership of society, Herzberg mentioned the case of a company chairman who advocated bringing ethics and religion into all business dealings and the free distribution in the United States Steel Corporation of Norman Vincent Peale's *Guideposts*. As the dominant institution of contemporary society he held that industry should be prepared to exert its all-powerful influence wisely: the above instances were straws in the wind, tokens that it would do so. Industry has indeed achieved immense power in the present stage of history but like its great predecessor, the Church, it is built upon the foundation of certain assumptions about the nature of man.

'A premise of this essay is that every society has to establish myths in order to sustain its institutional forms.' With these words, Herzberg introduces his discussion of the myths about man, which served as centrepieces in the self-justifying ideologies of 'dominant societal bodies'. These myths also meet the cognitive needs of mankind at a rudimentary level. 'One of the reasons they are necessary and accepted is that man has a basic need to fill in the gaps in his understanding of the universe, and in particular man seeks to understand his place in the order of life.'

After a brief and almost mandatory reference to Freud as an authority, Herzberg turned to consider what he regarded as the two significant versions of the nature of man in the Bible: God's creation of Adam and his covenant with Abraham and Moses. He then discussed in turn the medieval, Renaissance, Reformation and Industrial Revolution myths of man.

According to Herzberg it was the Renaissance above all else that awakened the belief that earthly achievement was an important need for mankind. It represented a return to what he called the Abraham concept of mankind. By the end of the fifteenth century secularization had already set it, and gradually the hope of some heavenly salvation began to fade as modern man emerged from his psychological immaturity into a full consciousness of his own powers. He quoted with approval Pico della Mirandola's grandiloquent statement of man's power: 'To him it is granted to have whatever he chooses, to be whatever he will.'[1]

Herzberg was no historian, and most of his historical generalizations would not stand up to a critical scrutiny. For example, his virtual equation of the Renaissance with secular humanism ignores the fact that most humanists in that period did not doubt the truths of their Christian religion, including such doctrines as the fall of man and original sin. Humanists such as Erasmus, Colet and More experienced no conflict between their faith and the new learning. Although Herzberg was doubtless correct in discerning in the Renaissance a new emphasis upon man as creator as well as creature, more angel than beast, it was Christianity which mothered and cradled the advance. As Professor Dresden concluded in *Humanism in the Renaissance* (1968): 'It is this emphasis on man's potential within the Christian faith that gives humanism its authentic ring. With this object in view it takes up the strands of the past and weaves a new pattern.'

According to Herzberg — in good company this time — the Industrial Revolution spawned its own myth of 'economic man'. Two streams of tradition flowed into this river. The first of these tributaries was the so-called Protestant Ethic, which had only a tenuous link with Calvin's theology. Under the mantle of the Reformation, religious and moral sanctions were given to success in industry. Secondly, the social and philosophical literature stemming from Darwin's theory of evolution fed the river with a pseudo-scientific justification for economic success in terms of 'the survival of the fittest'. This and other related myths, such as 'mechanistic man' and 'social man', were used to justify particular ways of organizing work in factories. To these Herzberg added another myth, which he called 'neo-mechanistic' or 'instrumental man'. This represents the tendency towards greater intellectual specialization and less responsibility in management. All these myths, however, deal with only the Adam side of human nature, the animal needs for survival and the avoidance of pain.

Herzberg's own faith rested upon man's innate potentiality. 'This article of psychological faith gives purpose to man's existence.' Man's destiny is to grow by his own efforts into his full potential. Jung, Adler, Rogers, Goldstein and Maslow had all glimpsed this goal, but all had failed to define self-actualization or psychological growth. It is not fear of sin and punishment which constitute man's primary motivation but his compelling urge to realize his potential as a creative and unique individual, according to his own innate abilities and within the limits of reality, and this end he can achieve by a process of continuous psychological growth.

CHARACTERISTICS OF GROWTH

In contrast to Maslow, Herzberg related his discussion of the characteristics of psychological growth specifically to job capability and performance. He arranged them into two hierarchies: cognitive and motivational. At the bottom of the cognitive hierarchy stands *knowing more*, or the acquisition of new knowledge. The knowledge in question consists of new facts and principles necessary to deal with the unfamiliar part of the job. An observant and experienced supervisor can notice the attainment of this knowledge. Work should not be so structured or rationalized that the possibility of experiencing the unfamiliar is excluded altogether.

The second cognitive characteristic is *more relationships in knowledge*, or the integrating of new information into the corpus of previous knowledge. Herzberg saw this process typified in science: facts are uncovered and related to principles, which in turn are related to laws, and laws to theories. At the top of the cognitive hierarchy comes *creativity*, which is significantly given a very wide definition as 'any knowledge, understanding or principle that originates from the individual.' Herzberg mentions that the term 'insight' is sometimes used to convey this 'non-original' creativity by the individual. Although a concept may be common knowledge a person by insight makes it his own, and therefore he has grown.

Within Herzberg's general understanding of growth as realization of potentiality, creativity means using to the full the manufacturing abilities of people. Therefore jobs should include assignments which do not have built-in solutions or responses. 'Some people are determined; some are determiners. The determiners use their brains for dynamic, creative ability, while the determined are unable to do so.'

The fourth characteristic of growth (and the first in the motivational triad) is *effectiveness in ambiguity*. From the Abraham point of view the uncertainty and ambiguity of the world adds challenge, variety and opportunity to life: it can even be considered to be the reward for being human. Herzberg contrasts the childish preference for simple decisions between clearly marked alternatives with the adult necessity for making more important decisions from a greater number of possibilities, and assuming responsibility for the choice.

Herzberg's fifth characteristic is *individuation*, the process of becoming an individual. He implies that in America the complementary process of socialization has tended to swamp the area of individual response to life, a trend which is nothing less than 'partial suicide'. This point is illustrated by the way that personal identity is usually established by reference to membership of groups, e.g. 'I am an engineer' or 'I am a husband'. Herzberg regarded becoming an individual as one of 'the highest levels of psychological growth'. Working with others should not only produce results for that 'fictitious entity' the group, but also provide means for personal enhancement.

The sixth Herzberg characteristic of psychological growth is *real growth*. This clearly tautological statement meant for Herzberg that growth is not to be measured by job titles, appurtenances of rank, relationships with others and status symbols. Nor can it be augmented by claiming the growth of other people as one's own. 'All these factors,' wrote Herzberg in his summary of the six points of psychological growth, 'can be recognized as the Abraham view of man, that is, the necessity to realize the human potential for perfection. This is contrary to the Adam view of man, which sees the human being as characterized by the need to avoid physical deprivation.'

THE SOCIAL CONTEXT

Herzberg's concept of the nature of man must be set in the double context of the American society of the 1950s and 1960s, and the particular phase in the development of industry as symbolized by the Detroit car assembly lines. It was in part a protest against the uniformities imposed by the educational and social system on the one hand, and by the specialization of industrial labour on the other. In order to strengthen his case Herzberg had read his dualistic theory of human motivation into both the Bible and human history. Although his historical survey is inevitably over-simplified and therefore distorted, Herzberg — in company with Douglas McGregor and others — performed a valuable service by drawing attention to the persistence down the centuries of both the pessimistic and optimistic views of man. If F. W. Taylor was the equivalent of Hobbes in industry, then Herzberg stands firmly in the tradition of Locke.[2]

The Bible, with its vision of the grandeur and misery of man, obviously does not support the view that man is the most god-like being in the universe. The emergence of a doctrine of the divinity and self-perfectibility of man is rather a symptom of the decline of biblical and Christian religion. Herzberg's true intellectual progenitors were such nineteenth century figures as Feuerbach (1804–72) and Nietzsche (1844–1900). Certainly we can observe in Herzberg's writings some reflections of the Romantic movement's emphasis upon individualism, subjective experience, work as struggle and conquest, creativeness and 'joy through work'.[3] We may legitimately trace also the hedonism of such eighteenth century rationalists as Jeremy Bentham. But it is impossible to be certain of these inferences because so many hidden roots have nourished the syncretic humanism typified by Herzberg's book *Work and the Nature of Man*. Nor should we forget that his views contain and promote a doctrine of man and the place of work in life which is not far removed from what the Christian theologian has to say.

Herzberg, however, remains essentially a practical reformer, retailing his ideological patchwork of myths and philosophies in order to encourage certain changes in industry, reforms which others of different philosophical or religious persuasion would also regard as laudable. For a much more subtle picture of man we must turn back to Maslow.

9 Maslow's Self-Actualizing Man

It were no slight attainment could we merely fulfil what the nature of man implies.
Epictetus

In 1950 Professor Maslow published a paper entitled 'Self-Actualizing People: A Study of Psychological Health.' He had written it in 1943 but seven years elapsed 'before I summoned up enough courage to print it' in *Motivation and Personality*. The inherent methodological shortcomings of such a study 'not planned as an ordinary research . . . not a social venture but a private one, motivated by my own curiosity . . .' caused this scholarly hesitation, which Maslow only overcame by the exercise of intellectual courage: 'the only manly thing to do is not to fear mistakes, to plunge in, to do the best one can, hoping to learn enough from blunders to correct them eventually.' These remarks of Maslow in preface are important because they set the keynote and establish the status for his unique and valuable study in psychological health.

Maslow selected his subjects mainly from among personal friends or acquaintances, public and historical figures. A sample of university students produced only one suitable subject and a dozen or two possible ones for the future. For selection purposes subjects had to demonstrate freedom from identifiable personality disorders and some evidence of self-actualization, translated at this stage into 'the full use and exploitation of talents, capacities, potentialities, etc. . . They are people who have developed or are developing to the full stature of which they are capable. These potentialities may be either idiosyncratic or species-wide, so that the self in self-actualization must not have too individualistic a flavour.'

Maslow divided his 'cases' into three broad categories, each subdivided into anonymous contemporaries and named public or historical people. These divisions can be set out as follows:

	Cases	*Partial Cases*	*Potential or Possible Cases*
Acquaintances	5	5	20
	–	–	–
Public/Historical	Lincoln		G. W. Carver
	Jefferson	Walt Whitman	Eugene V. Debs
	Eleanor Roosevelt	Henry Thoreau	Albert Schweitzer
	Jane Addams	Beethoven	Thomas Eakins
	William James	F. D. Roosevelt	Fritz Kreisler
	Spinoza	Freud	Goethe

Based upon his informal conversations with the older 'acquaintances', more explicit interviews with the younger ones, and (presumably) a wide reading of the biographical literature, Maslow offered the following impressions of some eighteen distinctive characteristics of self-actualizing people.

1. *More efficient perception of reality and more comfortable relations with it*

Maslow noted such symptoms as an unusual capacity to detect the spurious, fake or dishonest in personality, and to judge people correctly. More generally, in art and music for example, the subjects seemed able to see concealed or confused realities more swiftly and correctly than others. Maslow preferred to call this 'perception of something that was absolutely there' rather than mere good taste or a set of subjective opinions.

Secondly, the healthy subjects accepted and liked the unknown, ambiguous or unstructured. By contrast many intellectuals occupy themselves exclusively with the known and familiar: 'polishing it, arranging and rearranging it, classifying it' instead of 'discovering'. The subjects sought truth not out of a catastrophic need for certainty, safety, definiteness, and order, and thus they could find in doubt and uncertainty a pleasurably stimulating challenge.

2. *Acceptance (self, others, nature)*

'It would convey the wrong impression to say that they are self-satisfied,' wrote Maslow. 'What we must say rather is that they can take the frailties and sins, weaknesses, and evils of human nature in the same unquestioning spirit with which one accepts the characteristics of nature.' Acceptance included a full acceptance of the natural bodily functions, with a corresponding lack of disgusts and aversions. There is not an absolute lack of guilt or shame, but these feelings centre on improvable shortcomings, 'stubborn remnants of psychological ill-health' (e.g. prejudice, jealousy, envy), and failings in the species, culture or group at large.

3. *Spontaneity*
Self-actualizing people are more spontaneous and unconventional in their inner lives than in their outward behaviour. Convention does not prevent them from doing what they regard as important, but they do not make a great issue about unimportant regulations or customs. 'Because of this alienation from ordinary conventions and from the ordinarily accepted hypocrisies, lies, and inconsistencies of social life, they sometimes feel like spies or aliens in a foreign land and sometimes behave so.'

Above all, self-actualizing people possess a motivational life different from that of ordinary people in a *qualitative* way. 'It seems that we must construct a profoundly different psychology of motivation for self-actualizing people, e.g. expression motivation, rather than deficiency motivation. Perhaps it will be useful to make a distinction between living and *preparing* to live. Perhaps the concept of motivation should apply *only* to non self-actualizers. Our subjects no longer strive in the ordinary sense, but rather develop. They attempt to grow to perfection and to develop more and more fully in their own style. The motivation of ordinary men is a striving for the basic need gratifications that they lack. But self-actualizing people in fact lack none of these gratifications; and yet they have impulses. They work, they try, and they are ambitious, even though in an unusual sense. For them motivation is just character growth, character expression, maturation, and development; in a word self-actualization.'

4. *Problem centring*
The subjects characteristically looked outwards. 'They generally are not problems for themselves and are not generally much concerned about themselves; e.g. as contrasted with the ordinary introspectiveness that one finds in insecure people. These individuals customarily have some mission in life, some task to fulfil, some problem outside themselves which enlists much of their energies.

'This is not necessarily a task that they would prefer or choose for themselves; it may be a task that they feel is their responsibility, duty or obligation. This is why we use the phrase "a task that they must do" rather than the phrase "a task that they want to do". In general these tasks are nonpersonal or unselfish, concerned rather with the good of mankind in general, or of a nation in general, or of a few individuals in the subject's family.

'With a few exceptions we can say that our subjects are ordinarily concerned with basic issues and external questions of the type that we have learned to call philosophical or ethical. Such people live customarily in the widest possible frame of reference. They seem never to get so close to the trees that they fail to see the forest. They work within a framework of values that are broad and not petty, universal and not local, and in terms of a century rather than a moment. In a word, these people are all in one sense or another philosophers, however homely.' Such an attitude of living *sub specie aeternitas* has dozens of implications for daily living, giving a sense of perspective which imparts a certain serenity and lack of worry over immediate concerns.

5. *The quality of detachment; the need for privacy*

The subjects like solitude and privacy to a markedly greater degree than average people. Maslow would not apply the dichotomy introvert-extrovert to them, but chose instead the term 'detachment' to describe a certain calmness, aloofness and dignity the self-actualizers possessed even in trying or undignified circusmtances. 'Perhaps this comes in part from their tendency to stick by their own interpretation of a situation rather than to rely upon what other people feel or think about the matter. This reserve may shade over into austerity and remoteness.'

6. *Autonomy; independence of culture and environment*

The self-actualizing person depends for his or her own development on his or her own resources: he or she does not find his or her main satisfactions in the external world or other people. Such independence contributes to their natural stoical endurance of blows, frustrations and deprivations.

7. *Continued freshness of appreciation*

The subjects retained their sensibility. They could respond to fresh manifestations of natural or artistic beauty.

8. *The mystic experience; the oceanic feeling*

Such experiences could be placed on a continuum from intense to mild. In the acute cases 'there were the same feelings of limitless horizons opening up to the vision, the feeling of being simultaneously more powerful and also more helpless than one ever was before, the feeling of great ecstasy and wonder and awe, the loss of placing in time and space with, finally, the conviction that something extremely important and valuable had happened, so that the subject is to some extent transformed and strengthened even in his daily life by such experiences.' In mild forms such mystic experiences may occur in the 'favoured' individual a dozen times a day. Maslow explicitly disassociated this feeling from any theological or supernatural reference, preferring Freud's descriptive phrase — 'the oceanic feeling'.

9. *Gemeinschaftsgefühl*
This term, introduced by Alfred Adler (1870–1937),[1] suggests a 'deep feeling of identification, sympathy, and affection, in spite of occasional anger, impatience, or disgust. . . Because of this they have a genuine desire to help the human race. It is as if they were all members of a single family.'

10. *Inter-personal relations*
Self-actualizing subjects tended to have deep and intense friendships, and their choice of friends is discriminating in favour of people like themselves. Close and exclusive personal relationships can co-exist with a wider humanitarian benevolence. 'The people *tend* to be kind or at least patient to almost everybody. They have an especially tender love for children and are easily touched by them. In a very real even though special sense, they love or rather have compassion for all mankind.

'This love does not lack discrimination. The fact is that they can and do speak realistically and harshly of those who deserve it, and especially of the hypocritical, the pretentious, the pompous, or the self-inflated.'

11. *The democratic character structure*
Such self-actualizing people are an élite of character, capacity, and talent rather than of birth, race, blood, name, family, age, youth, fame or power. They show a universal respect for *any* human being and a wide social friendliness. 'For instance they find it possible to learn from anybody who has something to teach them — no matter what other characteristics he may have. In such a learning relationship they do not try to maintain any

outward dignity or to maintain status or age prestige or the like. It should even be said that my subjects share a quality that could be called humility of a certain type. They are all quite well aware of how little they know in comparison with what *could* be known and what *is* known by others. . . They give this honest respect to a carpenter who is a good carpenter; or for that matter to anybody who is a master of his own tools or his own craft.'

12. *Discrimination between means and ends*
The subjects possessed definite moral standards. 'One way of expressing the quality I am trying to describe was suggested by Dr David Levy, who pointed out that a few centuries ago these would all have been described as men who walk in the path of God or as godly men. So far as religion is concerned, none of my subjects is orthodoxly religious, but on the other hand I know of only one who describes himself as an atheist (four of the total group studied). The few others for whom I have information hesitate to call themselves atheists. They say that they believe in a God, but describe this God more as a metaphysical concept than as a personal figure. Whether or not they could be called religious people as a group must then depend entirely on the concept or definition of religion that we choose to use. If religion is defined only in social-behavioural terms, then these are all religious people, the atheists included. But if more conservatively we use the term religion so as to include and stress the supernatural element and institutional orthodoxy (certainly the more common usage) then our answer must be quite different, for then almost none of them is religious.'

In general the subjects behave as though ends and means could be distinguished, and as if the former were more important than the latter. They also have the capacity for treating as ends-in-themselves some of the experiences and activities more normal people would regard as means to ends, e.g. a journey.

13. *Philosophical, unhostile sense of humour*
'One very early finding was quite easy to make, because it was common to all my subjects, was that their sense of humour is not of the ordinary type. They do not consider funny what the average man considers funny. Thus they do not laugh at hostile humour (making people laugh by hurting someone) or superiority humour (laughing at someone else's inferiority) or authority-rebellion humour (the unfunny, smutty joke). Characteristically

what they consider humour is most closely allied to philosophy than to anything else. . . Probably Lincoln never made a joke that hurt anybody else; it is also likely that many or even most of his jokes had something to say, had a function beyond just producing a laugh. They often seemed to be education in a more palatable form, akin to parables or fables. . . It should not be surprising that the average man, accustomed as he is to joke books and belly laughs, considers our subjects to be rather on the sober and religious side.'

14. *Creativeness*
'This is a universal characteristic of all the people studied or observed,' declared Maslow. 'There is no exception. Each one shows in one way or another a special kind of creativeness or originality or inventiveness that has certain characteristics.' In contrast to the 'special-talent' creativeness of a Mozart these people display a general creativeness akin to that which is evident in children. It bestows upon all they do a certain attitude or spirit: 'In this sense there can be creative shoemakers or carpenters or clerks.' Maslow believed that powerful sets of inhibitions normally damped down this natural spontaneity which reappeared in self-actualizing people. 'Perhaps when we speak of creativeness here we are simply describing from another point of view, namely, from the point of view of consequence, what we have described above as a greater freshness, penetration, and efficiency of perception.'[2]

15. *Resistance to enculturation*
By this phrase Maslow meant to convey the relative degree of acceptance and rejection of American cultural values by his sample of self-actualizing people.

16. *The imperfections of self-actualizing people*
Self-actualizing people exhibit many of what we could call the lesser human failings.

17. *Values and self-actualization*
Many moral conflicts disappear for the self-actualizing person. His or her other characteristics give him or her a firm foundation for a natural value system.

18. *The resolution of dichotomies in self-actualization*
In conclusion Maslow made perhaps one of his most important

generalizations about self-actualizing people, namely that 'what had been considered in the past to be polarities or opposites or dichotomies were so *only in unhealthy people*. In healthy people, these dichotomies were resolved, the polarities disappeared, and many oppositions thought to be intrinsic merged and coalesced with each other to form unities.

'For example the age-old opposition between heart and head, reason and instinct, or cognition and conation was seen to disappear in healthy people where they became synergic rather than antagonists, and where conflict between them disappears because they say the same thing and point to the same conclusion. In a word, in these people desires are in excellent accord with reason. St Augustine's "Love God and do as you will" can easily be translated, "Be healthy and then you may trust your impulses."

'The dichotomy between selfishness and unselfishness disappears altogether in healthy people because in principle every act is *both* selfish and unselfish. Our subjects are simultaneously very spiritual and very pagan and sensual. Duty cannot be contrasted with pleasure, nor work with play when duty *is* pleasure, when work *is* play, and the person doing his duty and being virtuous is simultaneously seeking his pleasure and being happy. If the most socially identified people are themselves also the most individual people, of what use is it to retain the polarity? If the most mature are also childlike? And if the most ethical and moral people are also the lustiest and most animal?

'Similar findings have been reached for kindness-ruthlessness, concreteness-abstractness, acceptance-rebellion, self-society, adjustment-maladjustment, detachment from others-identification with others, serious-humorous, Dionysian-Apollonian, introverted-extraverted, intense-casual, serious-frivolous, conventional-unconventional, mystic-realistic, active-passive, masculine-feminine, lust-love, and Eros-Agape. . .

'In this, as in other ways, healthy people are so different from average ones, not only in degree but in kind as well, that they generate two very different kinds of psychology. . . The study of self-actualizing people must be the basis for a more universal science of psychology.'

10 The Path to Self-Actualization

Sacrifice may be a flower that virtue will pluck on its road, but it was not to gather this flower that virtue set forth on its travels.
Maurice Maeterlinck

By painting self-actualization in such attractive colours Maslow stimulated the desire for it. But how could this enviable state of being be attained? He was aware that there was some relationship between the meeting of the lower needs and the emergence of the higher ones, but he knew that there was no necessary cause-and-effect relation between needs towards the upper end of the scale. Thus Maslow did not underwrite unlimited gratification of individual needs as the pathway to self-actualization. On the contrary, he argued that such a course would prove to be counter-productive, for one of the key characteristics of the self-actualizers was their capacity to tolerate frustration of the lower needs when the occasion demanded. Maslow praised self-restraint and self-discipline. But a reasonable gratification of the lower needs must be taken as a necessary condition for full self-actualization although it cannot guarantee it.

Also Maslow denied that self-actualization came solely through advancing years. There is no question of having to wait until the fifth and sixth decades of life before experiencing it, as the high average age of his sample might suggest. The urge towards self-actualization was a core characteristic of human nature at all stages of its development. But the *desire* for self-actualization and the *experience* of it are not all the same. If not by the gratification of all other needs, nor by the natural process of growing older, how does one reach the state of being a self-actualizing person?

THE ROCK OF SELF-CENTREDNESS

The difficulty at this point is that the desire for self-actualization appears to be fundamentally self-centred while the reality of self-actualization implies some form of transcendence of self. Is self-centredness the hidden rock upon which our strivings towards self-actualization will founder? It is hard to get a plus from a minus. Now Maslow was aware of the dilemma. He never wearied from repeating the paradox that in the self-actualized person the dichotomy between selfishness and unselfishness has been transcended. The self-actualizers are unselfish and other-centred, but they also possess a healthy regard for themselves, perhaps more than that of most people.

Eventually Maslow came to see that the phrase 'self-actualization' itself presented a stumbling-block which no amount of explanation could quite overcome: 'Besides being clumsy from a literary point of view, this term has proven to have the unforeseen shortcomings of appearing a) to imply selfishness rather than altruism, b) to slur the aspect of duty and of dedication to life tasks, c) to neglect the ties to other people and to society, and the dependence of individual fulfilment upon a "good society", d) to neglect the demand-character of non-human reality, and its intrinsic fascination and interest, e) to neglect egolessness and self-transcendence, and f) to stress, by implication, activity rather than passivity or receptivity. This has turned out to be so in spite of my careful efforts to describe the empirical *fact* that self-actualizing people are altruistic, dedicated, self-transcending, social, etc.'[1]

How far it is the language which is misleading, and how far the very concept of self-actualization itself, remains a matter for discussion. By substituting for it such terms as 'full-human-ness', or Being and Becoming, or even by inventing the neologism 'Eupsychia', Maslow sought to communicate what he regarded as the plain truth about human nature at its best. But having defined salvation so as to disinfect it from the charge of selfishness he still had to give a secular counterpart to the doctrine of salvation. And this was no academic question. Disciples began to arrive at Brandeis University to learn from the prophet of the secrets of new human-ness.

SALVATION THROUGH GOOD WORK

Maslow appears to have treated such seekers after salvation with some harshness. He professed to have little time for these 'research students' who wanted to work with him in the field of self-actualization studies in the hope that they would discover from him the way to salvation. In a subsequently published tape-recorded monologue, Maslow said:

> 'I have spoken about dilettantes, for instance (as contrasted with workers and doers), and indicated my contempt for them. I have mentioned how often I have tested people with these fancy aspirations simply by giving them a rather dull but important and worthwhile job to do. Nineteen out of twenty fail the test. I have learned not only to give this test but to brush them aside completely if they don't pass it. I have preached to them about joining the "League of Responsible Citizens" and down with the free-loaders, hangers-on, mere talkers, the permanent passive students who study forever with no results. The test of any person is — that you want to find out whether he's an apple tree or not — Does he bear apples? Does he bear fruit? That's the way you tell the difference between fruitfulness and sterility, between talkers and doers, between the people who change the world and the people who are helpless in it.'[2]

We may be sure that many of these 'students' came to find enlightenment rather than academic drudgery: they were disciples more than scholars. Many others, who made no pretence at scholarship, simply wanted to know how they could fulfil their unsatisfied longings for they knew not what. How could the 'Third Psychology' help them? In 1962, almost twenty years after his perceptive profile of the self-actualizing personality, Maslow gave his answer:

> 'Another point that has been coming up is the talk about personal salvation. For instance, at the Santa Rosa existential meetings there was much of this kind of talk, and I remember exploding in a kind of irritation and indicating my disrespect for such salvation seekers. This was on the grounds that they were selfish and did nothing for others

and for the world. Besides, they were psychologically stupid and psychologically incorrect because seeking for personal salvation is *anyway* the wrong road to personal salvation. The only real path, one that I talked about in my public lecture there, was the path set forth in the Japanese movie "Ikiru", i.e. salvation via hard work and total commitment to doing well the job that fate or personal destiny calls you to do, or any important job that "calls for" doing.

'I remember citing various "heroes", people who had attained not only personal salvation but the complete respect and love of everybody who knew them; all of them were good workers and responsible people, and furthermore all of them were as happy as was possible for them to be in their circumstances. This business of self-actualization via a commitment to an important job and to worthwhile work could also be said, then, to be the path to human happiness (by contrast with the direct attack or the direct search for happiness – happiness is an epiphenomenon, a by-product, something not to be sought directly but an indirect reward for virtue). The other way – of seeking for personal salvation – just doesn't work for anybody I have *ever* seen – that is the introspection, the full-time-in-a-cave all by one's self some place. This may work for people in India and Japan – I won't deny that – but I have never seen it work for anybody in all my experience in the United States. The only happy people I know are the ones who are working well at something they consider important. Also, I have pointed out in my lecture and in my previous writings that this was universal truth for all my self-actualizing subjects. They were meta-motivated by meta-needs (B-values)* expressed in their devotion to, dedication to, and identification with some great and important job. This was true for every single case.

Or I can put this very bluntly: *Salvation is a By-Product of Self-Actualizing Work and Self-Actualizing Duty*.'[3]

This passage suggests a confusion between two strands of thought in Maslow's remedy. In the first of these two themes Maslow seems to be recommending at least certain kinds of work

* i.e. 'Being'-values.

as the narrow gateway to salvation for all those seeking self-actualization. Commit yourself to some cause or service which is, you believe to be, more important than the state of your personality, he advises. The theologian may recognize in this prescription, if pushed to the extreme, a secular form of the doctrine of 'salvation through good works'.

The difficulty with it, as generations of seekers have found, is that self-centredness is too deeply ingrained in human nature (the doctrine of original sin) to yield to such a summons. For Maslow is saying little more than 'Be unselfish!' to a person whose self-concern is so acute that he is searching for some escape route from himself. Like the Mosaic Law in the experience of St Paul, such secular prescriptions may do more to reveal and activate innate selfishness than to cure it, although (like the Law) the destination they point to may not be in question. But we cannot travel far along the recommended route without falling prey to other forms of self-centredness (despair or pride) which may be worse than our first condition. However, that preliminary stage of the journey (and discovery) may be necessary.

Perhaps by making self-actualization so much the centre of his philosophy Maslow placed an added difficulty in front of those who must now simultaneously forget about themselves and yet choose 'self-actualizing Work and self-actualizing Duty'. Previously Maslow has firmly tied values to needs: what meets my higher needs has value for me. Therefore apparently the only criterion I can have in choosing work is how far it ministers to my self-actualization. Maslow can offer no other justification for self-forgetting work except the empirical observation that self-actualizing subjects do actually manifest such altruistic feelings. In other words, he bases a prescription upon a description.

We may not doubt that Maslow's self-actualized subjects shared the characteristic of deep involvement in good work of one kind or another. The issue, however, is whether or not this healthy work is the cause or effect of their state. If it is cause then Maslow's prescription holds good. If it is effect then the disciples might well and legitimately ask Maslow: 'Show me how I can *first* become a self-actualizing person so that I can then discover a cause and immerse myself in work, and express my new self in it.'

The second strand in Maslow's thought, however, suggests that there is some 'fate or personal destiny' which 'calls' a person to self-actualizing work and duty, or — additionally or alternatively — there is some important work and duty which 'calls for' doing. It is not the seeker who chooses some work which will lead, so he believes, to self-realization; on the contrary, some mysterious transcendent process (or the job itself) seems to choose him or her. This line of thought recalls the Christian concept of vocation and Maslow had no hesitation in using that word in its literal sense. The characteristic of self-actualizing people is that they have a vocational attitude to work in which 'work tends to be the same as play; vocation and avocation become the same thing'. For such fortunate people work has been transformed: 'When duty is pleasant and pleasure is fulfilment of duty, then they lose their separateness and oppositeness.' Maslow's subjects have therefore attained the objective pithily described by Robert Frost:

My object in living is to unite
My avocation and vocation
As my two eyes make one in sight.[4]

So far we have posed an either/or relationship between the two strands in Maslow's thought on salvation, but it is clear that he intuitively felt that *both* seeking and 'calling' are involved. The debate upon the relative emphasis upon the two aspects is reminiscent of the much older debates between St Augustine and Pelagius, Luther and medieval Catholicism. A study of Christian saints (the equivalent to Maslow's self-actualized people) would suggest that struggle, unhappiness, doubt and even despair often precede or accompany an experience of a 'call' from God which somehow answers all their needs and strivings. Christianity rejects both the extreme poles of Pelagianism and Quietism; it underwrites the search for solutions in some compound or mixture in the middle ground between self-help and grace. Quite how these combine defies analysis, as well for the theologian as for the psychologist.

Despite this recognition of the supra-personal dimension in self-actualization Maslow's own bias was towards the activist element in the compound. Perhaps for cultural and democratic reasons he expressed a confident belief that the way of self-actualization was open to all nations. Like most humanitarian reformers he tended to emphasize the practical steps which both individuals and society could take to realize the utopia of a world civilization founded upon self-actualization. The Chinese proverb, 'A journey of a thousand miles begins with a single step' aptly sums up the practical emphasis of his message.

Sooner or later, so Maslow believed, the thrust towards self-actualization would propel the pilgrim into the orbit of Being-values. These values – partly discovered in the unfolding self, partly received from the culture, partly chosen by conscious decisions – came into play to direct the flight path of self-actualization. In particular professional values (competence, service) would exert their influence:

> 'For any man of good will, there are a great variety of causes, or duties to dedicate himself to with equal satisfaction. One might say that this inner structure of human nature is cartilaginous rather than bony; or that it can be trained and guided like a hedge or even espaliered like a fruit tree.
>
> 'The problems of choice and renunciation still remain even though a good tester or therapist should be able soon to see in a general way what the talents and capacities and needs of the person are, and be able, e.g. to give him pretty decent vocational guidance.
>
> 'Furthermore, as the growing person dimly sees the range of fates from among which he can choose, in accordance with opportunity, with cultural praise or blame, etc., and as he gradually commits himself (chooses? is chosen?), let us say, to becoming a physician, the problems of self-making and self-creating soon emerge. Discipline, hard work, postponement of pleasure, forcing himself, moulding and training himself, all become necessary even for the "born physician". No matter how much he loves his work, there are still chores that must be swallowed for the sake of the whole.
>
> 'Or to put it another way, self-actualization via being a physician means being a *good* physician, not a poor one. This ideal certainly is partly created by him, partly given to him by the culture and partly discovered within himself. What he thinks a good physician ought to be is as determinative as his own talents, capacities and needs.'[5]

BEYOND SELF-ACTUALIZATION

His later writings suggest that Maslow had sensed the weakness of a philosophy which virtually equated the need for self-actualization with the purpose of life. He had glimpsed the necessity of going beyond self-actualization, and indeed the whole concept of needs, into a realm where values occupied a dual throne with needs. In the Preface to the second edition of *Toward a Psychology of Being*, written in 1968 shortly before his death, Maslow showed signs of wishing to break out of the system he had created, by affirming 'that I consider Humanistic, Third Force Psychology to be transitional, a preparation for a still "higher" Fourth Psychology, transpersonal, transhuman, centred in the cosmos rather than in human needs and interest, going beyond humanness, identity, self-actualization and the like.'

Quite what Maslow had in mind we shall never know. Certainly, however, the peripheral reality which he had not encompassed in his philosophy of self-actualization now had moved into the centre of the stage, for 'without the transcendent and the transpersonal we get sick, violent, and nihilistic, or else hopeless and apathetic. We need something "bigger than we are" to be awed by and to commit ourselves to in a new, naturalistic, empirical, non-churchly sense. . .'[6]

Maslow, it may be noted, had still not quite broken out of the framework of self-centred needs: God must be there because we need him. A Freudian could easily accuse him of wish-fulfilment. Supposing, however, God (in the full Hebraic-Christian sense of the term) does exist? What then happens to the concept of self-actualization and what difference does God's presence make to our natural motives for working?

CONCLUSION

How to Motivate Others: The Eight Rules of Motivation

Introduction

A man, woman or child is motivated when he or she WANTS to do something. Motivation covers ALL the reasons which cause a person to act, including negative ones like fear along with the more positive motives, such as money, promotion or recognition.

From the Fifty-Fifty Rule it follows that the extent to which you can motivate anyone else is limited. For fifty per cent of the cards are, so to speak, in their hands. You can provide motives or incentives in one way or another; you can offer rewards or issue threats; you can attempt to persuade. All these actual or potential influences may have an effect, for remember that fifty per cent of a person's motivation stems from the environment. If you are a manager-leader, then you are a key factor in the environment of those that work for you. But your power is limited. As the proverb says, 'You can take a horse to water, but you cannot make him drink.'

In this final section I have summed up what you CAN do under eight headings – the principles or rules of motivation. *HOW* you apply them will clearly depend upon the situation. But they stand as pillars of encouragement, both inviting you to take up your responsibility as a leader for inspiring others and pointing you in the right direction.

'I never saw a man in our profession . . . who possessed the magic art of infusing the same spirit into others which inspired their own actions . . . all agree there is but one Nelson.' So wrote Admiral Lord St Vincent to Nelson in a letter, a glowing tribute from such a superior to his junior. Will the same ever be said about you?

1. BE MOTIVATED YOURSELF

The first and golden rule of motivation is that you will never inspire others unless you are inspired yourself. Only a motivated leader motivates others. Example is the great seducer.

It is so simple and so obvious, isn't it? But why is it so neglected in management today?

Enthusiasm inspires, especially when combined with trust. Its key importance can perhaps best be seen by considering its opposites. What impression would we make as leaders if we were apathetic, stolid, half-hearted, indifferent and uninterested? Enthusiasm is infectious; and enthusiasts are usually competent too, since they believe in and like what they are doing.

One of the world's first philosopher-consultants, Confucius, was once called in by a Chinese feudal king to check the corruption and theft which was rife in his domain. The fact that both the king and his court indulged in these practices, and that others were taking their cue from them, soon became apparent to Confucius, and he simply pointed out to his client the motivating influence — for good or ill — of example. 'If you did not steal yourself,' he said, 'even if you rewarded men with gold to steal they would not do it.'

Before you criticize others for lack of motivation ask yourself if your own enthusiasm for and commitment to the task in hand is sincere, visible and tangible. Have you expressed it in deeds as well as words? Are you setting a good example? For motivation is caught, not taught.

Nothing great was ever achieved without enthusiasm.

Emerson

2. SELECT PEOPLE WHO ARE HIGHLY MOTIVATED

Since it is hard to motivate people who are not already motivated it makes sense to select those who already are. It is true that in the coldest flint there is hot fire, but you may lack the skill to release such hidden sparks.

You need people working for you who, like John Bunyan, 'could not be content, unless I was found in the exercise of my gift, unto which also I was greatly animated.' Bunyan added that 'great grace and small gifts are better than great gifts and no grace', which can be translated here to mean that when you select someone for a job a high motivation and modest talent is to be preferred to considerable talent but little or no evidence of motivation.

Given the absence of any reliable psychological tests to measure motivation, managers are thrown back on their judgement. Some useful tips for interviewers are:

- Remember that someone at an interview is trying to influence or motivate you to give them the job. Some people find it easy to *act* as if they are highly motivated or enthusiastic for an hour during an interview. Others, who may be very motivated, may come across as 'laid back'.
- By their fruits you shall know them. Look for evidence in what they have done. What someone wishes to do he will find a way of doing. Has persistence and perseverance – evidences of high motivation – ever been shown? Ask the referees who know him or her well.
- Describe several work situations that require high motivation and ask the applicant how they would react.

No man will find the best way to do a thing unless he loves to do that thing.

Japanese proverb

3. TREAT EACH PERSON AS AN INDIVIDUAL

Unless you ask a person what motivates them — what they want — you will not know. For we are all individuals. What motivates one person in the team may not motivate another. Enter into some sort of dialogue with each individual member of the group.

Not that individuals will always be clear about what they want. Our motivation changes with age and circumstance. One of your functions as a leader may be to help individuals to clarify what they are seeking at any given time in their careers.

A wise leader in an organization always remembers that a whole bushel of wheat is made up of single grains. By listening to individuals, giving them an opportunity to express their hopes and fears, the leader is also showing true care. The intention, however, must be to help if possible and not to manipulate. 'You would play upon me . . . You would seek to know my stops . . . You would pluck out the heart of my mystery'. That is cynical manipulation, as unmasked in Shakespeare's words.

Leadership stands in sharp contrast to such man-management. 'A good leader,' wrote Sir John Smythe VC, is 'someone whom people will follow through thick and thin, in good times and bad, because they have confidence in him as a person, his ability and his knowledge of the job, and because *they know they matter to him*.'

As many men, so many minds; every one in his own way.

Terence

4. SET REALISTIC AND CHALLENGING TARGETS

'There is no inspiration in the ideals of plenty and stability,' wrote John Lancaster Spalding. People are capable of transcending self in the pursuit of high and demanding ideals.

Most people reveal this capacity in the way they respond better to a challenge. There is a fine balance here. If objectives are totally unrealistic they will demotivate people; if they are too easy to attain, on the other hand, they are also uninspiring. As a leader you have to get the balance right. 'It is not enough to do our best,' said Winston Churchill. 'Sometimes we have to do what is required.'

In 3M, for example, managers are *challenged* by demanding goals. For instance, says Lewis W. Lehr, the former Chairman of 3M, in the field of innovation the targets are set to stretch all concerned:

> 'Our divisions shoot for a high target: In any given year, twenty five per cent of sales should come from products introduced within the last five years. Of course, not every division hits its target every year. But our managers are judged not only on their ability to make existing product lines grow but also on their knack for bringing innovative new products to market. So they have a built-in incentive to keep R&D strong.'

It is essential to AGREE targets or objectives with those who have to carry them out. For the principle is true that the more we *share* decisions which affect our working lives, the more we are motivated to carry them out. If the person *accepts* that the objective is both realistic and desirable or important, then he or she will start drawing upon *their* fifty per cent of the motivational equation.

> *By asking the impossible we obtain the best possible.*
>
> *Italian proverb*

5. REMEMBER THAT PROGRESS MOTIVATES

As the ACL model suggests, we are motivated not simply by our individual needs but also by needs emanating from the common task. We WANT to finish what we are doing. The more significant the task, the stronger is their need to complete it satisfactorily. John Wesley called it 'the lust to finish'.

It is a sound principle that progress motivates. If people know that they are moving forwards it leads them to increase their efforts. We invest more in success.

Therefore it is important to ensure that people receive proper feedback. Feedback is defined in Webster's Dictionary as 'the return to the input of a part of the output of a machine, system or process'. Without feedback people will not know if they are moving in the right direction at the right speed.

Conversely, feedback on relative lack of progress also motivates. For it concentrates minds on what must be done if success is to be yet achieved. If you confront people with the realities of their situation in this way, then the 'law of the situation' will do the work of motivation for you.

A man grows most tired while standing still.
Chinese proverb

6. CREATE A MOTIVATING ENVIRONMENT

Although you have limited power to motivate others you can do a great deal to create an environment which they will find motivating. Most of us have experienced the flip-side of such an environment: one that *reduces* motivation. A restrictive organizational culture, which over-emphasizes controls and reduces people to passive roles, coupled with an unpredictable and irascible superior who tells off people in public, is hardly likely to bring out the best in human nature.

It is important that Herzberg's 'hygiene' factors are properly catered for. The physical and psychological well-being of people has to have a top priority. Only introduce control systems where necessary, for over-controlling does reduce motivation. Double-check that people do have a proper input into the decisions that affect their working lives, especially when any substantial change is involved. Keep units or sub-units as small as possible, for large organizations tend to become bureaucratic and demotivational if they lack inspired leaders.

Lastly, pay attention to job design. Repetitive work can become boring if uninterrupted, so introduce as much variety as possible. Let people work on something they can recognize as their own product, for people find real autonomy motivates them. Ensure that the person doing the job understands its impact on others, so that they see the significance of it. That is vital, especially if you want people to be so involved that they contribute new ideas and help forward the essential process of innovation.

> *The creative act thrives in an environment of mutual stimulation, feedback and constructive criticism — in a community of creativity.*
>
> *William T. Brady*

7. PROVIDE FAIR REWARDS

A lynx chasing a snow rabbit will only chase it for about two hundred metres, then it gives up. For the food gained if the prey was caught will not replace the energy lost in the pursuit. Working on the same unconscious principle, it will chase a deer for longer.

All work implies this element of balancing what we give with what we expect to receive. Fairness or justice means that the return should be equivalent in value to the contribution. Performance ought to be linked to rewards, just as promotion should be related to merit.

The former – getting financial rewards fair – is easier said than done in many work situations. But the principle is still important and ways of applying it have to be found. Justinian wrote that 'Justice is the constant and unceasing will to give everyone his right or due.' That genuine and sustained intention is expected from any leader who has discretion over the distribution of rewards.

The principle has to be applied with especial care over monetary remunerations, for if fairness is not *perceived* there it can breed a lack of motivation and low morale. When remuneration is poor, workers put less effort into their jobs. Money is a key incentive. Therefore proper job evaluation schemes, involving a representative group of work people in the judgements about the financial worth of jobs, is vitally important.

There are, of course, other rewards we gain from working, as Maslow's hierarchy of needs illustrates. Opportunities for professional development and personal growth are especially valuable to good people. But money has a strategic importance for most people, not least as a measure of recognition for the significance of their contributions. As the means of exchange and as a store of wealth, money is probably the most useful material reward you can give.

He who likes cherries soon learns to climb.
German proverb

8. GIVE RECOGNITION

Despite what I have just written about money I believe that recognition is often an even more powerful motivator. As I hinted, money anyway often means more to people as a tangible symbol of recognition than as the wherewithal to buy more material goods.

This thirst for recognition is universal. In gifted people it amounts to a desire for fame or glory. For example, Isambard Brunel could write in his diary: 'My self-conceit and love of glory, or rather approbation, vie with each other which shall govern me.'

As a leader you can give recognition and show appreciation in a variety of ways. A sincere 'well done' or 'thank you' can work wonders for a person's morale.

But it is equally important to encourage a climate where each person recognizes the worth or value of the contribution of other members of the team. For it is recognition by our peers — discerning equals or colleagues — that we value even more than the praise of superiors. We are social animals and we thirst for the esteem of others. Without fairly regular payments by others into that deposit account it is hard to maintain the balance of our own self-esteem.

Seize every opportunity, then, to give recognition, even if it is only for effort. We cannot always command results. Perceive the worth of what the other person is doing and show your appreciation. You do not have to be a manager to do that, for true leadership can always be exercised from marginal positions.

Any of us will put out more and better ideas
if our efforts are fully appreciated.
Alexander F. Osborn

SUMMARY: HOW TO MOTIVATE OTHERS

1. BE MOTIVATED YOURSELF
2. SELECT PEOPLE WHO ARE HIGHLY MOTIVATED
3. TREAT EACH PERSON AS AN INDIVIDUAL
4. SET REALISTIC AND CHALLENGING TARGETS
5. REMEMBER THAT PROGRESS MOTIVATES
6. CREATE A MOTIVATING ENVIRONMENT
7. PROVIDE FAIR REWARDS
8. GIVE RECOGNITION

Those who are near will not hide their ability, and those who are distant will not grumble at their toil. . . That is what is called being a leader and teacher of men.

Hsün Tzu

Notes

Chapter One

1. A. H. Maslow, *Motivation and Personality* (New York, Harper and Brothers, 1954).
2. F. Herzberg, B. Mausner and B. B. Snyderman, *The Motivation to Work* (New York, John Wiley, 2nd edit., 1959) and F. Herzberg, *Work and the Nature of Man* (Cleveland, USA, World Publishing Company, 1966).
3. R. Tannenbaum and W. H. Schmidt, 'How to Choose a Leaderhship Pattern', *Harvard Business Review*, March–April (1958).
4. For confirmation of this point in particular, and for a discussion of sharing decisions in general, see F. A. Heller, *Managerial Decision-making: A Study of Leadership Styles and Power Sharing*, (Tavistock Publications, 1971).

Chapter Two

1. A. H. Maslow, *Eupsychian Management: A Journal* (Richard D. Irwin, 1965).
2. F. E. Fiedler, 'Leadership – A new model', *Discovery*, (April 1965) and, *A Theory of Leadership Effectiveness*, McGraw-Hill, (1967). For an appraisal, see W. Hill, 'An Empirical Test of Fiedler's Contingency Model of Leadership Effectiveness in Three Organizations', *The Southern Journal of Business, (July 1969)*. See also, R. Blake and J. Mouton, *The Management Grid*, Houston, Gulf Publishing, (1964). For further examples of the situationalist approach, see Bavelas, 'Leadership: Man and Function', *Administrative Science Quarterly*, 5, (1960), 491–498, and Bales and Slater, 'Role Differentiation in Small Decision-Making Groups', in Talcott Parsons, *et al., Family, Socialization and Interaction Process*, Glencoe: Free Press, (1955). For the origins of the 'styles' preoccupation (in the work of Kurt Lewin), see Lewin and Lippitt, 'An Experimental Approach to the Study of Autocracy and Democracy: A Preliminary Note', *Sociometry*, 1, (1938), 292–300.
3. P. Hersey and K. H. Blanchard, *Management of Organizational Behaviour* (Englewood Cliffs, NJ, Prentice-Hall, 4th edit. 1982).

Chapter Three

1. N. Rudd, *T. E. Page*, Bristol Classical Press, 1983.

Chapter Four

1. *Motivation and Personality* (1954), p. ix. All the Maslow quotations in this chapter are from this book.
2. J. C. Smuts, *Holism and Evolution* (1926), p. ix.

Chapter Five

1. C. N. Cofer & M. H. Appley, *Motivation: Theory and Practice* (1964).
2. *The Human Side of Enterprise*, chapters 3 and 4.
3. R. Likert, *New Patterns of Management* (1961).
4. C. Argyris, *Personality and Organization* (1957) and *Integrating the Individual and the Organization (1964).*
5. *J. H. Goldthorpe, et al., The Affluent Worker* (1968), p. 178.
6. M. D. Vernon, *Human Motivation* (1969), p. 161.
7. A. Fox, *A Sociology of Work in Industry* (1971), p. 10; cf. Professor J. Morris of Manchester Business School, 'The Human Meaning of Work' (unpublished paper, 1971): the important question is whether the instrumental attitude 'be established as a norm for future action or seen as a tragic sign of failed aspirations' (Reported in *The Times*, 18 January 1971).

Chapter Six

1. F. Herzberg, B. Mausner, R. Peterson, and D. Capwell, *Job Attitudes: Review of Research and Opinion* (1957).
2. *Motivation and Personality*, pp. 64–65, 81. Cp. Maslow's nearest approach to Herzberg's position: 'The parallel contrast in the motivational life of a single person is between growth motivation and defence motivation (homeostasis, safety motivation, the reduction of pains and losses, etc.), *Eupsychian Management* (1965), p. xii.
3. For example, Professor Liam Hudson was aware of his own tendency towards dichotomy: 'It is evident that I think in binary terms, and of tension between opposing values. This may prove a gross oversimplification. . . My hope of course is that there is enough in nature and the human mind that is polar to make my approach worth pursuing. If not, I can only throw up my hands — a binary beast — and leave the field to minds more subtle,' *Frames of Mind* (1968), p. 93.
4. Others have noted the basic compatibility of the two approaches. For example, in *Work and the Nature of Man* (1968), pp. 140–41, Herzberg described a doctoral study by one of his students who had applied the motivation-hygiene theory, using a modified form of Maslow's hierarchy, to thirty rehabilitation patients in a Cleveland hospital.
5. *Work and the Nature of Man*, p. 146; R. B. Ewen, 'Some Determinants of Job Satisfaction', *Journal of Applied Psychology*, Vol. 48 (1964); P. Wernimont and M. Dunnette, 'Intrinsic and Extrinsic Factors in Job Satisfaction', *Ibid.*, Vol. 50 (1966).
6. Herzberg cited the following references: V. A. Yadov, 'The Soviet

and American Worker: Job Attitudes', *Soviet Life, January 1965; A. Zdravomyslov and V. A. Yadov, 'A Case Study of Attitude to Labour',* *Problems of Philosophy*, Vol. 4 (Moscow, 1964).

7. M. S. Myers, 'Who are Your Motivated Workers', *Harvard Business Review*, Vol. 42 (1964), pp. 75–88.
8. K. Davis and G. R. Allen, 'Length of Time that Feelings Persist for Herzberg's Motivational and Maintenance Factors', *Personal Psychology*, Vol. 23 (1970).
9. G. Gunn, J. Veroff & S. Feld, *Americans View Their Mental Health* (1959); S. H. Peres, 'An Exploration of Engineers' and Scientists' Motives as Related to Job Performance', *American Psychological Association* (1963); H. Rosen, 'Occupational Motivation of Research Workers and Development Personnel', *Personnel Administration*, Vol. 26 (1963); M. R. Malinovsky & J. R. Barry, 'Determinants of Work Attitudes', *Journal of Applied Psychology*, Vol. 49 (1965); R. B. Ewen, C. L. Hulin, P. C. Smith & E. A. Locke, 'An Empirical Test of Herzberg's Two-Factor Theory', *ibid.*, Vol. 50 (1966); C. A. Lindsay, E. Marks & L. Gorlow, 'The Herzberg Theory: A Critique and Reformulation', *ibid.*, Vol. 51 (1967); G. B. Graen, 'Testing Traditional and Two-Factor Hypotheses Concerning Job Satisfaction', *ibid.*, Vol. 52 (1968); W. W. Ronan, 'Relative Importance of Job Characteristics', and 'Individual and Situational Variables Relating to Job Satisfaction, *ibid.*, Vol. 54 (1970).
10. *A Sociology of Work in Industry* (1971), p. 23.
11. R. J. Burke, 'Are Herzberg's Motivators and Hygienes Unidimensional?', *Journal of Applied Psychology*, Vol. 50 (1966); D. A. Wood & W. K. LeBold, 'The Multivariate Nature of Professional Job Satisfaction', *Personnel Psychology*, Vol. 23 (1970).
12. R. Payne, 'Factor Analysis of a Maslow-Type Need Satisfaction Questionnaire', *Personnel Psychology*, Vol. 25 (1970).
13. R. Wild, A. B. Hill and C. C. Ridgeway, 'Job Satisfaction and Labour Turnover amongst Women Workers', *The Journal of Management Studies*, Vol. 7 (1970).

Chapter Seven

1. *An Inquiry into the Nature and Causes of the Wealth of Nations* (1976), p. 7.
2. Cited by J. Ward, 'The Ideal of Individualism', in *The Business Establishment*, ed. E. Cheit (1967), p. 66.
3. See, for instance, chapter 3 'The Work of Elton Mayo', in J. A. C. Brown, *The Social Psychology of Industry: Human Relations in the Factory* (1954).

Chapter Eight

1. From *Orate de hominis dignitate*.
2. H. P. Knowles and B. O. Saxberg, 'Human Relations and the Nature of Man', *Harvard Business Review*, Vol. 45 (1967).

3. L. R. Furst, *Romanticism in Perspective* (1970); A. Tilgher, *Work: What it has meant to men through the ages* (1931).

Chapter Nine

1. A. Adler, *Social Interest* (1937). Adler thought that 'social interest' was nothing else than the old religious precept 'Love thy neighbour', P. Bottome, *Alfred Adler: Apostle of Freedom* (1937), p. 167. It came to be the centre-piece of his psychology: 'Social interest and social cooperation are therefore the salvation of the individual', A. Adler, *The Science of Living* (1930), p. 264.
2. *Motivation and Personality*, p. 224. For a fuller discussion of this aspect, see Maslow's essay 'Creativity in Self-Actualizing People', *Toward a Psychology of Being* (1968), pp. 135ff.

Chapter Ten

1. *Towards a Psychology of Being*, pp. 4, 163–4.
2. *Ibid.*, p. vi.
3. *Eupsychian Management*, p. 5.
4. *Ibid.*, pp. 5–6.
5. 'Two Tramps in Mud Time, or A Full-Time Interest', *Complete Poems* (1951), p. 305.
6. *Toward a Psychology of Being*, pp. 175–76.

Further Reading

Adler, A., *Social Interest: A Challenge to Mankind* (Trans. J. Linton & R. Vaughan), Faber and Faber, 1937.

——*The Science of Living*, George Allen and Unwin, 1930.

Alderfer, A., *Existence, Relatedness and Growth: Human Needs in Organizations*, New York, Free Press, 1972.

Arendt, H., *The Human Condition*, University of Chicago, 1958.

Argyris, C., *Personality and Organization: the Conflict between System and the Individual*, Harper and Row, 1957.

——*Integrating the Individual and the Organization*, Wiley, 1964.

Barnes, M. C., Fogg, A. H., Stephens, C. N. and Titman, L. G., *Company Organization: Theory and Practice*, George Allen and Unwin, 1970.

Berger, P. L. (ed.), *The Human Shape of Work: Studies in the Sociology of Occupations*, Macmillan, 1964.

Blauner, R., *Alienation and Freedom: The Factory Worker and his Industry*, University of Chicago, 1964.

Blum, M. L. and Naylor, J. C., *Industrial Psychology*, New York, Harper and Row, 1968.

Borne, E. and Henry, F., *A Philosophy of Work* (Trans. F. Jackson), Sheed and Ward, 1938.

Bottome, P., *Alfred Adler: Apostle of Freedom*, Faber and Faber, 3rd edit. 1957.

Brown, J. A. C., *The Social Psychology of Industry: Human Relations in the Factory*, Penguin, 1954.

Burns, T. (ed.), *Industrial Man*, Penguin, 1969.

Campbell, J. P., and others, *Managerial Behaviour, Performance and Effectiveness*, McGraw-Hill, 1970.

Child, J., *British Management Thought: a Critical Analysis*, George Allen and Unwin, 1969.

Cofer, C. N. and Appley, M. H., *Motivation: Theory and Practice*, Wiley, 1964.

Edholm, O. G., *The Biology of Work*, Weidenfeld and Nicolson, 1967.

Emmet, D., *Function, Purpose and Powers: Some Concepts in the Study of Individuals and Societies*, Macmillan, 1958.

Ford, R. N., *Motivation through Work Itself*, American Management Association, 1969.

Fox, A., *A Sociology of Work in Industry*, Collier-Macmillan, 1971.

Fraser, R. (ed.), *Work: Twenty Personal Accounts*, Penguin, 1954.

Friedmann, G., *The Anatomy of Work: the Implications of Specialization*, Heinemann, 1961.

Fromm, E., *Marx's Concept of Man*, Frederick Ungar, 1961.

Furst, L. R., *Romanticism in Perspective*, Macmillan, 1970.

Gardner, J. W., *Self-Renewal: The Individual and the Innovative Society*, Harper and Row, 1963.

Gellerman, S. W., *Motivation and Productivity*, American Management Association, 1963.

——*Management by Motivation*, American Management Association, 1968.

Goldstein, K., *The Organism*, American Book, 1939.

——*Human Nature in the Light of Psychopathology*, Harvard University Press, 1940.

Goldthorpe, J. H., Lockwood, D., Bechhofer, F. and Platt, J., *The Affluent Worker: Industrial Attitudes and Behaviour*, Cambridge University Press, 1968.

Gough, J. W., *The Rise of the Entrepreneur*, Batsford, 1969.

Goyder, G., *The Responsible Company*, Blackwell, 1961.

Gunn, G., Veroff, J. and Feld, S., *Americans View Their Mental Health*, Basic Books, 1959.

Hahn, C. P., *Dimensions of Job Satisfaction and Career Motivation*, Pittsburg, American Institute of Research, 1959.

Herzberg, F., Mausner, B., Peterson, R. and Capwel, D., *Job Attitudes: Review of Research and Opinion*, Psychological Service of Pittsburg, 1957.

Herzberg, F., Mausner, B. and Snyderman, B. B., *The Motivation to Work*, John Wiley and Sons, 1959 (2nd edition).

Herzberg, F., *Work and the Nature of Man*, London, Stapels Press, 1968. (Published in America in 1966).

Ivens, M. (ed.), *Industry and Values: The Objectives and Responsibilities of Business*, Harrap, 1970.

Jung, C., *Modern Man in Search of a Soul*, Harcourt, Brace & Co., 1933.

——*The Integration of the Personality*, Routledge and Kegan Paul, 1950.

Katz, D. and Kahn, R. L., *The Social Psychology of Organizations*, Wiley, 1978 (2nd edit.).

Klein, L., *The Meaning of Work*, The Fabian Society, 1963.

Lamont, C., *The Philosophy of Humanism*, Barrie & Rockliff, 5th edit., 1965.

Lawler, E. E., *Motivation in Work Organizations*, Brooks–Cole, 1973.

Likert, R., *New Patterns of Management*, McGraw-Hill, 1961.

Lubac, H. de, *The Drama of Atheist Humanism*, Sheed and Ward, 1947.

Lupton, T., *On the Shop Floor*, Pergamon, 1963.

——*Management and the Social Sciences*, Hutchinson, 1966.

Macmurray, J., *The Self as Agent* and *Persons in Relation*, Faber and Faber, 1957 and 1961. Gifford Lectures, 1953–54.

Maslow, A. H., *Motivation and Personality*, Harper and Row, 1954.

——(ed.), *New Knowledge in Human Values*, Harper and Bros, 1959.

——*Religions, Values, and Peak-Experiences*, Ohio State University Press, 1964.

——*Toward a Psychology of Being*, Van Nostrand Reinhold, (2nd edit.), 1968.

——*Eupsychian Management: A Journal*, Richard D. Irwin and the Dorsey Press, 1965.

Mayo, E., *The Human Problems of an Industrial Civilization*, Macmillan, 1933.
_____*The Social Problems of an Industrial Civilization*, Harvard University Press, 1945.
McClelland, D. C. *et al.*, *The Achievement Motive*, Appleton-Century-Crofts, 1953.
McClelland, D. C., *The Achieving Society*, Van Nostrand, 1961.
McGregor, D., *The Human Side of Enterprise*, McGraw Hill, 1960.
O'Brien, R. H., Dickinson, A. M. and Rosow, M. P., *Industrial Behaviour Modification. A Learning-based Approach to Industrial Organizational Problems*, Pergamon, 1982.
O'Toole, J., *Work in America*, MIT Press, 1973.
Passmore, J., *The Perfectibility of Man*, Duckworth, 1970.
Paul, W. J. and Robertson, K. B., *Job Enrichment and Employee Motivation*, Gower Press, 1970.
Robertson, I. T., and Smith, M., *Motivation and Job Design: Theory, Research and Practice*, Institute of Personnel Management, 1985.
Roethlisberger, F. J. and Dickson, W. J., *Management and the Worker*, Harvard University Press, 1959.
Rogers, C., *Counselling and Psychotherapy*, Houghton Mifflin, 1942.
_____*Client Centered Therapy*, Houghton Mifflin, 1951.
_____*On Becoming a Person: A Therapist's View of Psychotherapy*, London, Constable, 1961.
Sayles, L. R., *Behaviour of Industrial Work Groups*, John Wiley, 1958.
Schacht, R., *Alienation*, Allen and Unwin, 1971.
Schein, E. H., *Organizational Psychology*, Englewood Cliffs, NJ, Prentice-Hall, 1980.
Smigel, E. O. (ed.), *Work and Leisure: A Contemporary Social Problem*, New Haven (Connecticut), College and University Press, 1963.
Steers, R. M. and Porter, L. W., *Motivation and Work Behavior*, New York, McGraw-Hill, 1979.
Tannenbaum, A. S., *Social Psychology of the Work Organization*, California, Wadsworth; and London, Tavistock, 1966.
Tilgher, A., *Work: What it has meant to men through the ages* (trans. from Italian by D. C. Fisher), Harraps, 1931.
Turner, A. N. and Lawrence, P., *Industrial Jobs and the Worker*, Harvard University Press, 1965.
Vernon, M. D., *Human Motivation*, Cambridge University Press, 1969.
Vroom, V. H., *Work and Motivation*, John Wiley, 1964.
Weick, K. E., *The Social Psychology of Organizing*, Addison–Wesley, 1979.
Whyte, W. F., *Men at Work*, Irwin and Dorsey, 1961.
_____*Money and Motivation*, Harper and Bros, 1955.

Index